Appalachian Trail Guide to New York-New Jersey

Appalachian Trail Guide to New York-New Jersey

New York-New Jersey Trail Conference

Daniel D. Chazin
Field Editor

Thirteenth Edition

Appalachian Trail Conference
Harpers Ferry

Guidebook Contributors

Daniel D. Chazin, Editor
Walter Daniels
Paul DeCoste
Ronald J. Dupont, Jr.
Jane Geisler
Stephen Klein
Anne Lutkenhouse
George Muller
Ron Rosen
Weiland Ross
Glenn Scherer
Art Schneier
Peter Senterman

Cover photo of the Lemon Squeezer, Harriman State Park, New York.
© 1994 Michael Warren

© 1994 New York-New Jersey Trail Conference,
New York, New York

Published by The Appalachian Trail Conference,
Harpers Ferry, West Virginia

ISBN 0-917953-55-X

Thirteenth Edition
Printed in the United States of America on recycled paper.

Contents

Notice to All Trail Users

The information contained in this publication is the result of the best effort of the publisher, using information available to it at the time of printing. Changes resulting from maintenance work and relocations are constantly occurring and, therefore, no published route can be regarded as precisely accurate at the time you read this notice.

Notices of pending relocations are indicated. Maintenance of the Trail is conducted by volunteers and the maintaining clubs listed in this guidebook. Questions about the exact route of the Trail should be addressed to the Editor, *Appalachian Trail Guide to New York-New Jersey*, New York-New Jersey Trail Conference, G.P.O. Box 2250, New York, N.Y. 10116, (212) 685-9699. On the Trail, please pay close attention to—and follow—the white blazes and any directional signs.

Responsibility for Safety

It is extremely important to plan your hike, especially in places where water is scarce. Purify water drawn from any source. Water purity cannot be guaranteed. The Appalachian Trail Conference and the various maintaining clubs attempt to locate good sources of water along the Trail but have no control over these sources and cannot, in any sense, be responsible for the quality of the water at any given time. You must determine the safety of all water you use.

Certain risks are inherent in any Appalachian Trail hike. Each A.T. user must accept personal responsibility for his or her safety while on the Trail. The Appalachian Trail Conference and its member maintaining clubs cannot ensure the safety of any hiker on the Trail, and, when undertaking a hike on the Trail, each user thereby assumes the risk for any accident, illness, or injury that might occur on the Trail.

Enjoy your hike, but please take all appropriate precautions for your safety and well-being.

Safety and Security

Although criminal acts are probably less common on the Appalachian Trail than in most other human environments, they do occur. Crimes of violence, including murder and rape, have taken place over the years. It should be noted, however, that such serious crimes on the A.T. have a frequency rate on the order of fewer than one per year, on a trail that enjoys three to four million visitors in the same period. Even if such events are less common on the Trail than elsewhere, they can be more difficult to deal with because of the remoteness of most of the Trail. When hiking, you must assume the need for at least the same level of prudence as you would exercise if walking the streets of a strange city or an unknown neighborhood.

A few elementary suggestions can be noted. Above all, it is best not to hike alone. Be cautious of strangers. Be sure that family and/or friends know your planned itinerary and timetable. If you customarily use a "Trail name," your home contacts should know what it is. Although telephones are rarely handy along the Trail, if you can reach one, dial "911" or ask the operator to connect you to the state police if you are the victim of, or a witness to, a crime.

The carrying of firearms is **not** recommended. The risks of accidental injury or death far outweigh any self-defense value that might result from arming oneself. In any case, guns are illegal on national parklands and in certain other jurisdictions as well.

Be prudent and cautious, without allowing common sense to slip into paranoia.

How to Use This Guide

The Trail data in this guide have been divided into 18 New York-New Jersey sections separated by highway crossings or other geographical features. The sections generally cover no more than a day's travel on the Trail. In addition, this guide includes a description of the southernmost Trail section in Connecticut, designated Connecticut Section Six. Part of that section passes through New York and is also designated New York Section One. The northernmost Trail section entirely in New York is designated New York Section Two.

The chapters for each Trail section are divided into three or four parts. The first part includes general information needed primarily for planning. This material is arranged under individual headings in the following order:

Brief Description of Section
Road Approaches
Public Transportation
Maps
Shelters and Campsites
Supplies and Services
Public Accommodations

The detailed "Trail Description," the actual guide to the footpath, follows in two parts. Data are given first for walking south on the Trail and then for walking north. Trail data are presented in both directions of travel so hikers do not have to mentally reverse Trail descriptions. A column of distances on the left gives the mileage from the start of the section to important points along the Trail. Each point (such as stream crossings, shelters, summits, or important turns) is briefly described, followed by directions to the next point.

After some of the sections, a short chapter gives information on important side trails. If many side trails cross the A.T. in a certain area, no attempt has been made to describe them all. Rather, the reader is referred to other publications that describe trails in the area in more detail.

Six maps, based on USGS topographic quadrangles with additional cartography by the New York-New Jersey Trail Conference and the Appalachian Trail Conference, are included with this volume. In some sections, other available maps are also listed. It should be noted that, due to many recent relocations, the route of the A.T. is often shown incorrectly on unadjusted USGS topographic maps and on other commercially available maps.

The Appalachian Trail

The Appalachian Trail (A.T.) is a continuous, marked footpath extending more than 2,150 miles along the crest of the Appalachian mountain range from Katahdin, a granite monolith in the central Maine woods, south along the crest of the Appalachian mountain range to Springer Mountain in Georgia.

The Trail traverses mostly public land in 14 states. Virginia has the longest section, with 541 miles, while West Virginia has the shortest, almost 26 miles along the Virginia-West Virginia boundary and a short swing into Harpers Ferry at the Maryland border. The highest elevation along the Trail is 6,643 feet at Clingmans Dome in the Great Smoky Mountains. The Trail is 124 feet above sea level near its crossing of the Hudson River in New York.

Credit for establishing the Trail belongs to three leaders and countless volunteers. The first proposal for the Trail to appear in print was an article by regional planner Benton MacKaye of Shirley Center, Massachusetts, entitled, "An Appalachian Trail, a Project in Regional Planning," in the October 1921 issue of the *Journal of the American Institute of Architects*. He envisioned a footpath along the Appalachian ridgeline where urban people could retreat to nature.

MacKaye's challenge kindled considerable interest, but, at the time, most of the outdoor organizations that could participate in constructing such a trail were east of the Hudson River. There were four existing trail systems that could be incorporated into an A.T. The Appalachian Mountain Club (AMC) maintained the excellent series of trails in New England, but most ran north-south; the Trail could not cross New Hampshire until the chain of huts built and operated by the AMC permitted an east-west alignment. In Vermont, the southern 100 miles of the Long Trail, then being developed in the Green Mountains, were connected to the White Mountains by the trails of the Dartmouth Outing Club.

In 1923, a number of area hiking clubs that had formed the New York-New Jersey Trail Conference opened the first new section of the A.T. in the Harriman-Bear Mountain State Parks.

The Appalachian Trail Conference (ATC) was formed in 1925 to stimulate greater interest in MacKaye's idea and coordinate the clubs' work in choosing and building the route. The Conference remains a nonprofit educational organization of individuals and clubs of volunteers dedicated to maintaining, managing, and protecting the Appalachian Trail.

Although interest in the Trail spread to Pennsylvania and New England, further work was not completed until 1926, when retired Judge Arthur Perkins of Hartford, Connecticut, began persuading more groups to locate and cut the footpath through the wilderness. His enthusiasm provided the momentum that carried the Trail idea forward.

The southern states had few trails and even fewer clubs. The "skyline" route followed by the A.T. in the south was developed largely within national forests. A number of clubs were formed in various parts of the southern Appalachians to take responsibility for the Trail there.

Judge Perkins, ATC chairman from 1927 to 1930, interested Myron H. Avery in the Trail. Avery, chair of the Conference from 1931 to 1952, enlisted the aid and coordinated the work of hundreds of volunteers. The Trail was completed on August 14, 1937, when a Civilian Conservation Corps crew opened the last section (on the ridge between Spaulding and Sugarloaf mountains in Maine).

At the eighth meeting of the ATC, in June 1937, Conference member Edward B. Ballard successfully proposed a plan for an "Appalachian Trailway" that would set apart a buffer on each side of the Trail, dedicated to the interests of those who travel on foot.

Steps taken to effect this long-range protection program culminated first in an October 15, 1938, agreement between the National Park Service and the U.S. Forest Service for the promotion of an Appalachian Trailway through the relevant national parks and forests, extending one mile on each side of the Trail. Within this zone, no new parallel roads would be built or any other incompatible development allowed. Timber cutting would not be permitted within 200 feet of the Trail. Similar agreements, creating a zone one-quarter-mile in width, were signed with most states through which the Trail passes.

After World War II, the encroachments of highways, housing developments, and summer resorts caused many relocations, and the problem of maintaining the Trail's wilderness character became more severe. ATC members turned to Congress and President Lyndon B. Johnson for help.

In 1968, Congress established a system of national scenic trails and designated the Appalachian Trail and the Pacific Crest Trail as the initial components. The National Trails System Act directs the secretary of the interior, in consultation with the secretary of agriculture, to administer the Appalachian Trail primarily as a footpath and protect the Trail against incompatible activities, including the use of motorized vehicles. Provision was also made for acquiring rights-of-way for the Trail, both inside and outside the boundaries of federally administered areas.

In 1970, supplemental agreements under the act—among the National Park Service, the U.S. Forest Service, and the Appalachian Trail Conference—established the specific responsibilities of these organizations for initial mapping, selection of rights-of-way, relocations, maintenance, development, acquisition of land, and protection of a permanent Trail. Agreements also were signed between the park service and the various states, encouraging them to acquire and protect a right-of-way for the Trail outside federal land.

Slow progress of federal efforts and lack of initiative by some states led Congress to strengthen the National Trails System Act. President Jimmy Carter signed the "Appalachian Trail amendment" on March 21, 1978.

The new legislation emphasized the need for protecting the Trail, including acquiring a corridor, and authorized $90 million for that purpose. With less than 45 miles unprotected by 1994, this part of the project is expected to be completed by the end of this decade.

In 1984, the Interior Department delegated the responsibility for managing the A.T. corridor lands outside established parks and forests to the Appalachian Trail Conference. The Conference and its clubs retain primary responsibility for maintaining the footpath, too. A new, more comprehensive 10-year agreement was signed in 1994.

The Conference is governed by a volunteer Board of Managers, consisting of a chair, three vice chairs, a treasurer, a secretary, a corresponding secretary, and 18 members, six from each of the three regions of the ATC: New England, mid-Atlantic, and southern.

The Conference membership consists of organizations that maintain the Trail or contribute to the Trail project and individuals. ATC membership provides a subscription to *Appalachian Trailway News*, published five times a year, and 15-percent discounts on publications. The Conference also issues two newsletters: *The Register*, for

Trail maintainers, and *Trail Lands*, for contributors to its land-trust program, the Trust for Appalachian Trail Lands.

The Conference publishes information on constructing and maintaining hiking trails, official A.T. guides, general information on hiking and trail use, and other Trail-related books. Annual membership dues range from $18 to $30, with life memberships available for $500 (individual) or $750 (couple). Membership forms and a complete list of publications are available from the Appalachian Trail Conference, P.O. Box 807, Harpers Ferry, W. Va. 25425; (304) 535-6331. The office is open from nine a.m. to five p.m. (Eastern time) Monday through Friday and nine to four on weekends from mid-May through October.

The New York-New Jersey Trail Conference

The New York-New Jersey Trail Conference (NY-NJ TC) is a nonprofit volunteer organization that maintains the Appalachian Trail from the Connecticut border to the Delaware Water Gap. In 1923, founders of the NY-NJ TC constructed and opened the first section of the A.T. in Harriman-Bear Mountain State Parks, N.Y. Through a network of more than 80 local hiking clubs and more than 9,000 individual members, volunteers continue to maintain this section of the Trail as well as other trails in New York and New Jersey.

The NY-NJ TC was formed in 1920 when local hiking clubs gathered to plan a system of marked trails to make Harriman-Bear Mountain State Parks more accessible to the public. During the 1930s, more trails were built, and a system of trail maintenance was developed, giving each hiking club a share of the responsibility. Today, this network covers more than 1,000 miles of marked trails from the Catskills and Taconics south to the Delaware Water Gap.

In addition to maintaining the A.T. in New York and New Jersey and managing federal Trail lands there, the NY-NJ TC is responsible for relocating the Trail away from roads and unprotected private lands and onto protected woodlands. Of the more than 160 miles of the Trail in New York and New Jersey, 55 miles have been relocated since 1978 into a protected corridor approximately 1,000 feet wide. The NY-NJ TC, ATC, and state and federal officials have entered into cooperative agreements and adopted local management plans for the Trail that define the obligations and responsibilities of all parties. The relocations in these two states have made the A.T. through New York and New Jersey a hike you won't want to miss.

In addition to trail-building and maintenance, NY-NJ TC volunteers devote many hours to other projects and issues affecting the trails. Every spring, the conference sponsors "Litter Day," a massive effort to clean trash out of our woods. The conference also supports the enactment and implementation of "bottle bills" to reduce litter along the trails. In addition, the conference protects woodlands, wildlife, and places of scenic beauty. For example, the conference is working with other environmental groups to prevent major development in Sterling Forest in New York that would destroy the natural beauty of the area.

NY-NJ TC publications include the *New York Walk Book, Guide to the Long Path, Harriman Trails: A Guide and History, Hiking the Catskills, Circuit Hikes in Northern New Jersey, Hiking Guide to Delaware Water Gap National Recreation Area,* and maps for Harriman-Bear Mountain State Parks, North Jersey Trails, East Hudson Trails, South Taconic Trails, Kittatinny Trails, West Hudson Trails, Hudson Palisades, Pyramid Mountain, High Mountain, Shawangunks, and Catskills. The first five of those map sets cover sections of the A.T. The NY-NJ TC also publishes the *Trail Walker,* a bimonthly newspaper for members that includes information on A.T. relocations in the two states. Members also receive a publications discount.

For further information, write or call the New York-New Jersey Trail Conference, G.P.O. Box 2250, New York, N.Y. 10116; (212) 685-9699.

General Information

Trail Marking

The Appalachian Trail is marked for travel in both directions. The marks are white-paint blazes about two inches wide and six inches high on trees, posts, and rocks. Occasionally, on open ledges, stone cairns identify the route. In some areas, diamond-shaped A.T. metal markers or other signs mark the Trail. Two blazes, one above the other, signal an obscure turn, a change in route, or a warning to check blazes carefully. In New York and New Jersey, the upper of the two blazes indicating a turn is offset in the direction of the turn.

When the route is not obvious, normal marking procedure is to position the blazes so that anyone standing at one blaze will always be able to see the next. When the footway is unmistakable, blazes frequently are farther apart. If you have gone a quarter-mile without seeing a blaze, retrace your steps until you locate one, and then check to ensure that you did not miss a turn. Since the Trail is marked for both directions, a glance back may locate blazes in the opposite direction.

Side trails from the A.T. to water, viewpoints, and shelters usually are blazed in blue paint. Intersecting trails not part of the A.T. are blazed in a variety of colors.

At trail junctions or near important features, the Trail route is sometimes marked by signs, too. Some list mileages and include detailed information.

Trail Relocations

Always follow the marked Trail. If it differs from the guidebook's Trail description, it is because the Trail was relocated recently in the area, probably to avoid a hazard or undesirable feature or to remove it from private property. If you use the old Trail, you may be trespassing, as well as generating ill will toward the Trail community.

Information on relocations between guidebook revisions often is available from ATC. Relocation information may also be obtained by consulting the bimonthly *Trail Walker*, published by the New York-New Jersey Trail Conference. Do not follow new trails that are not blazed, because they may not be open to the public yet.

Water

In many areas, water sources along the Trail are unsafe for drinking, and a considerable distance may pass before potable water can be obtained. Carrying a canteen is necessary; a two-quart minimum capacity is recommended. The exertion of hiking, combined with water shortages, could lead to dehydration, increase fatigue, and jeopardize an otherwise enjoyable experience.

Although the A.T. may have sources of clean, potable water, any water source can become polluted. Most water sources along the Trail are unprotected and consequently susceptible to contamination. *All* water should be purified by boiling, chemical treatment, or filtering before using. Take particular care to protect the purity of all water sources. Never wash dishes, clothes, or hands in the water source. Make sure food and human wastes are buried well away from any water source.

Equipment

The basic equipment rule is, never carry more than you need.

Some items should be with you on every hike: the *A.T. Data Book* and/or guidebooks and maps; canteen; flashlight, even on day trips; whistle; emergency food; tissues; matches and fire starter; multipurpose knife; compass; rain gear; proper shoes and socks; warm, dry spare clothes; and a first-aid kit (see page 24).

Take the time to consult periodicals, books, employees of outfitter stores, and other hikers before choosing the equipment that is best for you.

Navigation

The compass variation, or declination, in New York and New Jersey varies from 13 degrees at the Connecticut-New York line to 11 degrees at the New Jersey-Pennsylvania line. This means that true north varies from 11 to 13 degrees to the right of the direction indicated by the compass needle, depending upon the location of the hiker. This is a significant variation that should be taken into account when the hiker orients himself or his map. The approximate compass declination at different points along the Trail is shown on each map accompanying this guide. Due to iron deposits in the area immediately west of the Hudson River (New York Sections Ten to Thirteen and New Jersey Section One), compass readings in this area may not be dependable.

Parking

Park in designated areas. If you leave your car parked overnight unattended, you may be risking theft or vandalism. Please do not ask Trail neighbors for permission to park your car near their homes.

Pests

Rattlesnakes and other poisonous snakes may be seen along the Trail in New York and New Jersey. See page 22 for the recommended treatment of snakebites.

Ticks, chiggers, no-see-ums, mosquitoes, and other insects may also be encountered. Hikers should carry insect repellent. To help prevent insect bites, hikers may wish to wear long pants, tucked into their socks. Some ticks may carry Lyme Disease. For information on the symptoms of Lyme disease, see page 20.

Poison ivy and other irritating plants grow along some sections of the Trail in New York and New Jersey. In some areas, particularly where the Trail goes through open fields (such as in New Jersey Section Three), vegetation grows rapidly in spring and summer, and, although volunteers try to keep the Trail cleared, some places may be filled by midsummer with dense growth. Use care in finding the Trail route where it may have become obscured by vegetation.

Hunting

Hunting is prohibited on all National Park Service lands, whether or not acquired specifically for the protection of the Appalachian Trail. However, in some cases, the boundary lines that identify these lands have not yet been surveyed, and it may be difficult for hunters to know that they are on NPS Trail lands. Hunting is permitted in New Jersey state parks (except in High Point State Park north of Deckertown Turnpike). In New York, hunting is prohibited in the state parks traversed by the A.T. (except in Depot Hill State Forest). The prudent hiker, especially in the fall, makes himself aware of local hunting seasons and wears blaze orange while hiking during times when hunting is allowed.

Getting Lost

Stop, if you have walked more than a quarter-mile (1,320 feet, or roughly five minutes of hiking) without noticing a blaze or other Trail indicator (see page 6). If you find no indication of the Trail, retrace your course until one appears. The cardinal mistake behind unfortunate experiences is insisting on continuing when the route seems obscure or dubious. Haste, even in a desire to reach camp before dark, only complicates the difficulty. When in doubt, remain where you are, to avoid straying farther from the route.

Hiking long distances alone should be avoided. But, if undertaken, it requires extra precautions. A lone hiker who suffers a serious accident or illness might be risking death if he has not planned for the remote chance of isolation. Your destinations and estimated times of arrival should be known to someone who will initiate inquiries or a search if you do not appear when expected. On long trips, reporting your plans and progress every few days is a wise precaution.

A lone hiker who loses his way and chooses to bushwhack toward town runs considerable risks if an accident occurs. If he falls helpless away from a used trail, he might not be discovered for days or even weeks. Lone hikers are advised to stay on the Trail (or at least on a trail), even if it means spending an unplanned night in the woods in sight of a distant electric light. Your pack should always contain enough food, water, and protective clothing to sustain you until daylight, when a careful retracing of your steps might lead you back to a safe route.

Distress Signals

The standard call for distress consists of three short calls, audible or visible, repeated at regular intervals. A whistle is particularly good for audible signals. Visible signals may include, in daytime, light flashed with a mirror or smoke puffs; at night, a flashlight or three small bright fires.

Anyone recognizing such a signal should acknowledge with two calls—if possible, by the same method—then go to the distressed person to determine the nature of the emergency. Arrange for additional aid, if necessary.

Most of the A.T. is used enough that, if you are injured, you can expect to be found. However, if an area is remote and the weather is inclement, fewer hikers will be on the Trail. In that case, it might be best to study the guidebook or map for the nearest place people are likely to be and attempt to move in that direction. If it is necessary to leave a heavy pack behind, be sure to take essentials, in case your rescue is delayed. In bad weather, a night in the open without proper covering could be dangerous.

Transportation to the Trail

Both the northern and southern ends of nearly all sections of the A.T. in New York and New Jersey are easily accessible by highways. The only exceptions are New York Section Thirteen and New Jersey Section One, which end at the New York-New Jersey state boundary rather than at roads. In addition, many other roads intersect the Trail in the middle of sections.

Bus or rail transportation is available to many end points of Trail sections or to nearby communities. Information on available public transportation is included in the general information preceding the Trail description for each section.

If no other transportation is available, you may wish to hitchhike. In New York, hitchhiking is prohibited on the roadway, defined as the travel portion of the highway between the outside white lines. Outside the roadway, hitchhiking is permitted, provided a dangerous situation is not created. In New Jersey, hitchhiking is legal only when the person soliciting the ride is completely off the highway, including the shoulder. Hitchhiking is prohibited along interstate highways in both states.

Group Hikes and Special Events

Special events, group hikes, or other group activities that could degrade the Appalachian Trail's natural or cultural resources or social values should be avoided. Examples of such activities include publicized spectator events, commercial or competitive activities, or programs involving large groups.

The policy of the Appalachian Trail Conference is that groups planning to spend one or more nights on the Trail should not exceed 10 people, and day-use groups should not exceed 25 people at any one location, unless the local maintaining organization or state agency has made special arrangements to both accommodate the group and protect Trail values.

The Hiker's Responsibilities

While virtually all of the land for a permanent Trail corridor has been acquired in New York and New Jersey, a few sections of the footpath are still on private property. In all cases, the land the Trail crosses must be respected and treated with care. Only careful use and respect will preserve the natural beauty of the Trail environment and ensure the integrity of the Appalachian Trail. Improper use can endanger the continuity of the Trail. Private landowners can promptly order hikers off their property and close the Trail route. Vandalism, camping and fires where they are prohibited, and other abusive use may result in Trail closure. Hikers should respect their natural surroundings and the property rights of landowners along the Trail.

Do not cut, deface, or destroy trees, flowers, mushrooms, or any other natural or man-made features.

Do not damage fences or leave gates open.

Do not litter the Trail or campsites. Carry out all trash; do not bury it for animals to discover.

Respect the privacy of those who live near the Trail. Approach homes along the Trail only during emergencies.

Do not carry firearms; they are of no use along the Trail.

Build fires only where permitted. Be careful with fire. Extinguish all burning material.

Keep to the defined Trail. Cutting across switchbacks, particularly on graded trails, disfigures the Trail, complicates route-finding, and causes erosion. The savings in time or distance are minimal; the damage is great. In areas where log walkways, steps, or rock treadway indicate special trail construction, take pains to use them. These have been installed to reduce trail-widening and erosion.

Dogs are often a nuisance to other hikers. The territorial instincts of dogs often result in fights with other dogs. Dogs also frighten some hikers and chase wildlife. If a pet cannot be controlled, it should be left at home; otherwise, it will generate ill-will toward the Appalachian Trail and its users. Also, many at-home pets' muscles, foot pads, and sleeping habits are not adaptable to the rigors of A.T. hiking.

In short, take nothing but pictures, leave nothing but footprints. Keep the wilderness, however near it might be to "civilization," a place of quiet and spiritual renewal.

The Route of the Appalachian Trail in New York and New Jersey

The southbound Appalachian Trail crosses the Connecticut-New York state line for the final time at Hoyt Road. It passes through Fahnestock State Park and continues southwest to the Bear Mountain Bridge.

After crossing the Hudson River, the Trail direction is west for southbound hikers and east for northbound hikers. In Harriman State Park, the Trail uses a portion of the original route established in 1923 and then follows the ridges of Bellvale and Bearfort mountains west of Greenwood Lake, where it enters New Jersey.

Following a newly constructed route on a protected corridor acquired largely by the State of New Jersey, the A.T. runs nearly parallel to the state line until it reaches High Point State Park, where it turns nearly southward and continues into Stokes State Forest. From here to the Delaware River, it generally follows the ridge line of the Kittatinny Mountains, sometimes on state land and sometimes through the Delaware Water Gap National Recreation Area. It crosses the Delaware River on the I-80 toll bridge at the gap.

First Aid Along the Trail

By Robert Ohler, M.D., and the
Appalachian Trail Conference

Hikers encounter a wide variety of terrain and climatic conditions along the Appalachian Trail. Prepare for the possibility of injuries. Some of the more common Trail-related medical problems are briefly discussed below.

Preparation is key to a safe trip. If possible, every hiker should take the free courses in advanced first aid and cardiopulmonary-resuscitation (CPR) techniques offered in most communities by the American Red Cross.

Even without this training, you can be prepared for accidents. Emergency situations can develop. Analyses of serious accidents have shown that a substantial number originate at home, in the planning stage of the trip.

Think about communications. Have you informed your relatives and friends about your expedition: locations, schedule, and time of return? Has all of your equipment been carefully checked? Considering the season and altitude, have you provided for water, food, and shelter?

While hiking, set your own comfortable pace. If you are injured or lost or a storm strikes, stop. Remember, your brain is your most important survival tool. Inattention can start a chain of events leading to disaster.

If an accident occurs, treat the injury first. If outside help is needed, at least one person should stay with the injured hiker. Two people should go for help and carry notes on the exact location of the accident, what has been done to aid the injured, and what help is needed.

The injured will need encouragement, assurances of help, and confidence in your competence. Treat him gently. Keep him supine, warm, and quiet. Protect him from the weather with insulation below and above him. Examine him carefully, noting all possible injuries.

General Emergencies

Back or neck injuries: Immobilize the victim's entire body where he lies. Protect head and neck from movement if the neck is injured, and treat as a fracture. Transportation must be on a rigid frame, such as a litter or door. The spinal cord could be severed by inexpert handling. This type of injury must be handled by a large group of experienced personnel. Obtain outside help.

Bleeding: Stop the flow of blood by using a method appropriate to the amount and type of bleeding. Exerting pressure over the wound with the fingers, with or without a dressing, may be sufficient. Minor arterial bleeding can be controlled with local pressure and bandaging. Major arterial bleeding might require compressing an artery against a bone to stop the flow of blood. Elevate the arm or leg above the heart. To stop bleeding from an artery in the leg, place a hand in the groin, and press toward the inside of the leg. Stop arterial bleeding from an arm by placing a hand between the armpit and elbow and pressing toward the inside of the arm.

Apply a tourniquet only if you are unable to control severe bleeding by pressure and elevation. *Warning: This method should be used only when the limb will be lost anyway.* Once applied, a tourniquet should only be removed by medical personnel equipped to stop the bleeding by other means and to restore lost blood. The tourniquet should be located between the wound and the heart. If there is a traumatic amputation (loss of hand, leg, or foot), place the tourniquet two inches above the amputation.

Blisters: Good boot fit, without points of irritation or pressure, should be proven before a hike. Always keep feet dry while hiking. Prevent blisters by responding early to any discomfort. Place adhesive tape or moleskin over areas of developing redness or soreness. If irritation can be relieved, allow blister fluid to be reabsorbed. If a blister forms and continued irritation makes draining it necessary, wash the area with soap and water and prick the edge of the blister with a needle that has been sterilized by the flame of a match. Bandage with a sterile gauze pad and moleskin.

Dislocation of a leg or arm joint is extremely painful. Do not try to put it back in place. Immobilize the entire limb with splints in the position it is found.

Exhaustion is caused by inadequate food consumption, dehydration and salt deficiency, overexertion, or all three. The victim may lose motivation, slow down, gasp for air, and complain of weakness, dizziness, nausea, or headache. Treat victim by feeding, especially carbohydrates. Slowly replace lost water (normal fluid intake should be two to four quarts per day). Administer salt dissolved in water (one teaspoon per cup). In the case of overexertion, rest is essential.

Fractures of legs, ankles, or arms must be splinted before moving the victim. After treating wounds, use any available material that will offer firm support, such as tree branches or boards. Pad each side of the arm or leg with soft material, supporting and immobilizing the joints above and below the injury. Bind the splints together with strips of cloth.

Shock should be anticipated after all injuries. It is a potentially fatal depression of body functions and becomes more critical with improper handling, cold, fatigue, and anxiety. Relieve the pain of the injury as quickly as possible. Do not administer aspirin if severe bleeding is present; Tylenol or another nonaspirin pain reliever is safe to give. Look for nausea, paleness, trembling, sweating, or thirst. Lay the hiker flat on his back, raise his feet slightly, or position him, if he can be safely moved, so his head is facing down the slope. Protect him from the wind, and keep him as warm as possible. A campfire will help.

Sprains: Look or feel for soreness or swelling. Bandage, and treat as a fracture. Cool and elevate joint.

Wounds (except eye wounds) should be cleaned with soap and water. If possible, apply a clean dressing to protect the wound from further contamination.

Chilling and Freezing Emergencies

Every hiker should be familiar with the symptoms, treatment, and methods of preventing the common and sometimes fatal condition of *hypothermia*. Wind chill and/or body wetness, particularly aggravated by fatigue and hunger, can rapidly drain body heat to dangerously low levels. This often occurs at temperatures well above freezing. Shivering, lethargy, mental slowing, and confusion are early symptoms of hypothermia, which can begin without the victim's realizing it and, if untreated, can lead to death.

Always keep dry, spare clothing and a water-repellent windbreaker in your pack, and wear a hat in chilling weather. Wet clothing loses much of its insulating value, although polypropylene, synthetic pile, and wool are warmer than other fabrics when wet. Always, when in chilling conditions, suspect the onset of hypothermia.

Wind Chill Chart

Actual Temperature (°F)

		50	40	30	20	10	0	-10	-20	-30	-40	-50
		Equivalent Temperature (°F)										
Wind Speed (mph)	0	50	40	30	20	10	0	-10	-20	-30	-40	-50
	5	48	37	27	16	6	-5	-15	-26	-36	-47	-57
	10	40	28	16	4	-9	-21	-33	-46	-58	-70	-83
	15	36	22	9	-5	-18	-36	-45	-58	-72	-85	-99
	20	32	18	4	-10	-25	-39	-53	-67	-82	-96	-110
	25	30	16	0	-15	-29	-44	-59	-74	-88	-104	-118
	30	28	13	-2	-18	-33	-48	-63	-79	-94	-109	-125
	35	27	11	-4	-20	-35	-49	-67	-82	-98	-113	-129
	40	26	10	-6	-21	-37	-53	-69	-85	-100	-116	-132

This chart illustrates the important relationship between wind and temperature.

To treat this potentially fatal condition, immediately seek shelter, and warm the entire body, preferably by placing it in a sleeping bag and administering warm liquids to the victim. The addition and close proximity of another person's body heat may aid in warming.

A sign of *frostbite* is grayish or waxy, yellow-white spots on the skin. The frozen area will be numb. To thaw, warm the frozen part by direct contact with bare flesh. When initially frozen, a cheek, nose, or chin can often be thawed by covering with a hand taken from a warm glove. Superficially frostbitten hands sometimes can be thawed by placing them under armpits, on the stomach, or between the thighs. With a partner, feet can be treated similarly. Do not rub frozen flesh.

Frozen layers of deeper tissue beneath the skin are characterized by a solid, "woody" feeling and an inability to move the flesh over bony prominences. Tissue loss is minimized by rapid rewarming of the area in water slightly below 105 degrees Fahrenheit (measure accurately with a thermometer).

Thawing of a frozen foot should not be attempted until the patient has been evacuated to a place where rapid, controlled thawing can take place. Walking on a frozen foot is entirely possible and does not cause increased damage. Walking after thawing is impossible.

Never warm over a stove or fire. This "cooks" flesh and results in extensive loss of tissue.

Treatment of a deep freezing injury after rewarming must be done in a hospital.

Heat Emergencies

Exposure to extremely high temperatures, high humidity, and direct sunlight can cause health problems.

Heat cramps are usually caused by strenuous activity in high heat and humidity, when sweating depletes salt levels in blood and tissues. Symptoms are intermittent cramps in legs and the abdominal wall and painful spasms of muscles. Pupils of eyes may dilate with each spasm. The skin becomes cold and clammy. Treat with rest and salt dissolved in water (one teaspoon of salt per glass).

Heat exhaustion, caused by physical exercise during prolonged exposure to heat, is a breakdown of the body's heat-regulating system. The circulatory system is disrupted, reducing the supply of blood to vital organs such as the brain, heart, and lungs. The victim can have heat cramps and sweat heavily. Skin is moist and cold with face flushed, then pale. Pulse can be unsteady and blood pressure low. Victim may vomit and be delirious. Place the victim in shade, flat on his back, with feet elevated 8-12 inches higher than head. Administer sips of salt water—half a glass every 15 minutes—for about an hour. Loosen his clothes. Apply cold cloths.

Heat stroke and *sun stroke* are caused by the failure of the heat-regulating system to cool the body by sweating. They are life-threatening emergencies. Body temperature can rise to 106 degrees or higher. Symptoms include weakness, nausea, headache, heat cramps, exhaustion, rapidly rising body temperature, pounding pulse, and high blood pressure. The victim may be delirious or comatose. Sweating will stop before heat stroke becomes apparent. Armpits may be dry and skin flushed and pink, turning ashen or purple in later stages. Move victim to a cool place immediately. Cool the body in any way possible (*e.g.* sponging). Body temperature must be regulated artificially from outside of the body until the heat-regulating system can be restored. Be careful not to overchill once his temperature goes below 102 degrees.

Heat weakness: Symptoms are fatigue, headache, mental and physical inefficiency, heavy sweating, high pulse rate, and general weakness. Drink plenty of water, find as cool a spot as possible, keep quiet, and replenish salt loss.

Sunburn causes redness of the skin, discoloration, swelling, and pain. It occurs rapidly and can be severe at higher elevations. It can be prevented by applying a commercial sun screen; zinc oxide is the most effective. Treat by protecting from further exposure and covering the area with ointment and a dressing. Give the victim large amounts of fluids.

Artificial Respiration

Artificial respiration might be required when an obstruction constricts the air passages or after respiratory failure caused by air being depleted of oxygen, electrocution, drowning, or toxic gases in the air. Quick action is necessary if the victim's lips, fingernail beds, or tongue have become blue, if he is unconscious, or if the pupils of his eyes become enlarged. If food or a foreign body is lodged in the air passage and coughing is ineffective, try to remove it with the fingers. If the foreign body is inaccessible, grasp the victim from behind. With one hand, hold the opposite wrist just below the breastbone. Squeeze rapidly and firmly, expelling air forcibly from the lungs, to expel the foreign body. Repeat this maneuver two to three times, if necessary.

If breathing stops, administer artificial respiration, as air can be forced around the obstruction into the lungs. The mouth-to-mouth, or mouth-to-nose, method of forcing air into the victim's lungs should be used. The preferred method is:

1. Clear the victim's mouth of any obstructions.
2. Place one hand under the victim's neck, and lift.
3. Place heel of other hand on the forehead, and tilt head backwards. (Maintain this position during procedure.) Use thumb and index finger to pinch nostrils.
4. Open your mouth, and make a seal with it over victim's mouth. If the victim is a small child, cover both the nose and the mouth.
5. Breathe deeply, and blow out about every five seconds, or 12 breaths a minute.
6. Watch victim's chest for expansion.
7. Listen for exhalation.

Poison Ivy

Poison ivy is the most common plant found along the Trail that irritates the skin. It is most often found as a vine trailing near the ground or climbing on fences or trees, sometimes up to 20 feet from the ground. A less common variety that is often unrecognized is an erect shrub, standing alone and unsupported, up to 10 feet tall.

The leaves are in clusters of three, the end leaf with a longer stalk and pointed tip, light green in spring but darkening as the weeks pass. The inconspicuous flowers are greenish; the berries, white or cream. The irritating oil is in all parts of the plant, even in dead plants, and is carried in the smoke of burning plants. Those who believe themselves immune may find that they are seriously susceptible if the concentration is great enough or the toxins are ingested.

If you have touched poison ivy, wash immediately with strong soap (but not with one containing added oil). If a rash develops in the next day or so, treat it with calamine lotion or Solarcaine. Do not scratch. If blisters become serious or the rash spreads to the eyes, see a doctor.

Lyme Disease

Lyme disease is contracted from bites of certain infected ticks. Hikers should be aware of the symptoms and monitor themselves and their partners for signs of the disease. When treated early, Lyme disease usually can be cured with antibiotics.

Inspect yourself for ticks and tick bites at the end of each day. The four types of ticks known to spread Lyme disease are smaller than the dog tick, about the size of a pin head, and not easily seen unless engorged. They are often called "deer ticks" because they feed on deer, a host for the disease, during one stage of their life cycle.

The early signs of a tick bite infected with Lyme disease are a red spot with a white center that enlarges and spreads, severe fatigue, chills, headaches, muscle aches, fever, malaise, and a stiff neck. However, one-quarter of all people with an infected tick bite show none of the early symptoms.

Later effects of the disease, which may not appear for months or years, are severe fatigue, dizziness, shortness of breath, cardiac irregularities, memory and concentration problems, facial paralysis, meningitis, shooting pains in the arms and legs, and other symptoms resembling multiple sclerosis, brain tumors, stroke, alcoholism, mental depression, Alzheimer's disease, and *anorexia nervosa*.

Some doctors are not yet well informed about the disease and can misdiagnose the symptoms. It may be necessary to contact a university medical center or other research center if you suspect you have been bitten by an infected tick.

A hiker who has contracted and been treated for the disease once should still take precautions. A vaccine is being worked on.

Lightning Strikes

Although the odds of being struck by lightning are low, 200 to 400 people a year are killed by lightning in the United States. Respect the force of lightning, and seek shelter during a storm.

Do not start a hike if thunderstorms are likely. If caught in a storm, immediately find shelter. Hard-roofed automobiles or large buildings are best; tents and convertible automobiles offer no protection. When indoors, stay away from windows, open doors, fireplaces, and large metal objects. Do not hold a potential lightning rod, such as a fishing pole. Avoid tall structures, such as ski lifts, flagpoles, powerline towers, and the tallest trees or hilltops. If you cannot enter a building or car, take shelter in a stand of smaller trees. Avoid clearings. If caught in the open, crouch down, or roll into a ball. If you are in water, get out. Spread out groups, so that everyone is not struck by a single bolt.

If a person is struck by lightning or splashed by a charge hitting a nearby object, the victim will probably be thrown, perhaps a great distance. Clothes can be burned or torn. Metal objects (such as belt buckles) may be hot. The victim often has severe muscle contractions (which can cause breathing difficulties), confusion, and temporary blindness or deafness. In more severe cases, the victim may have feathered or sunburst patterns of burns over the skin or ruptured eardrums. He may lose consciousness or breathe irregularly. Occasionally, victims stop breathing and suffer cardiac arrest.

If someone is struck by lightning, perform artificial respiration (see pages 19 and 20) and CPR until emergency technicians arrive or you can transport the injured to a hospital. Lightning victims may be unable to breathe independently for 15 to 30 minutes but can recover quickly once they can breathe on their own. Do not give up early; a seemingly lifeless individual can be saved if you breathe for him promptly after the strike.

If you come across someone who appears to have been struck, assume that the victim was thrown a great distance, protect the spine, treat other injuries, then transport him to the hospital.

Snakebites

Hikers on the Appalachian Trail may encounter copperheads or rattlesnakes on their journeys. These are pit vipers, characterized by triangular heads, vertical elliptical pupils, two or fewer hinged fangs on the front part of the jaw (fangs are replaced every six to ten weeks), heat-sensory facial pits on the sides of the head, and a single row of scales on the underbelly by the tail. Rattlesnakes have rattles on the tail.

The best way to avoid being bitten by snakes is to avoid their known habitats and reaching into dark areas (use a walking stick to move suspicious objects). Wear protective clothing, especially on feet and lower legs. Do not hike alone or at night in snake territory; always have a flashlight and walking stick. Do not handle snakes. A snake can bite and envenomate you with a reflex action for 20 to 60 minutes after its death.

Not all snakebites result in envenomation, even if the snake is poisonous. The signs of envenomation are one or more fang marks in addition to rows of teeth marks, burning pain, and swelling at the bite (swelling usually begins within five to ten minutes of envenomation and can become very severe). Lips, face, and scalp may tingle and become numb 30 to 60 minutes after the bite. (If these symptoms are immediate and the victim is frightened and excited, then they are most likely due to hyperventilation or shock.) Thirty to 90 minutes after the bite, the victim's eyes and mouth may twitch, and he may have a rubbery or metallic taste in his mouth. He may sweat, experience weakness, nausea, and vomiting, or faint one to two hours after the bite. Bruising at the bite usually begins within two to three hours, and large blood blisters may develop within six to 10 hours. The victim may have difficulty breathing, have bloody urine and vomit blood, and collapse six to 12 hours after the bite.

If someone you are with has been bitten by a snake, act quickly. The definitive treatment for snake-venom poisoning is the proper administration of antivenom. Get the victim to a hospital immediately.

Keep the victim calm. Increased activity can spread the venom and the illness. Retreat out of snake's striking range, but try to identify it. If you cannot do this easily, kill the snake with a blow to the head, and take it to the medical facility so the authorities can identify it and estimate the amount of antivenom necessary. (Remember to carry the snake in a container so that the jaws' reflex action cannot harm someone else.) Check for signs of envenomation.

Immediately transport the victim to the nearest hospital. If possible, splint the body part that was bitten, to avoid unnecessary motion. If a limb was bitten, keep it at a level below the heart. *Do not apply ice directly to the wound.* If it will take longer than two hours to reach medical help, and the bite is on an arm or leg, place a 2 x 2¼"-thick cloth pad over the bite and firmly wrap the limb (ideally, with an elastic wrap) directly over the bite and six inches on either side, taking care to check for adequate circulation to the fingers and toes. This wrap may slow the spread of venom.

First-Aid Kit

The following kit is suggested for those who have had no first-aid or other medical training. It costs about $20, weighs about a pound, and occupies about a 3" x 6" x 9" space.

Eight 4" x 4" gauze pads
Four 3" x 4" gauze pads
Five 2" bandages
Ten 1" bandages
Six alcohol prep pads
Ten large butterfly closures
One triangular bandage (40")
Two 3" rolls of gauze
Twenty tablets of aspirin-free pain-killer
One 15' roll of 2" adhesive tape
One 3" Ace bandage
Twenty salt tablets
One 3" x 4" moleskin
Snake-bite kit
Three safety pins
One small scissors
One tweezers
Personal medications as necessary

References

Red Cross first-aid manuals.
Mountaineering Medicine, by Fred T. Darvill, Jr., M.D., Wilderness Press, Berkeley, 1985.
Mountaineering First Aid: A Guide to Accident Response and First Aid, The Mountaineers, Seattle, 1985.
Emergency Survival Handbook, by the American Safety League, 1985. A pocket-sized book and survival kit with easy instructions.
Medicine for the Outdoors: A Guide to Emergency Medical Procedures and First Aid, by Paul S. Auerbach, M.D., Little Brown & Co., Boston, 1986.

Shelters and Campsites

The Appalachian Trail in New York and New Jersey has a number of shelters and campsites. In most cases, they are less than a day's hike apart. The following is a north-to-south list of the shelters and campsites along the Trail in New York and New Jersey. Additional information is provided in the Trail data for the respective sections of the Trail.

Trail Section	Miles from Conn.	Miles from Pa.	Shelter
NY 2	1.2	160.6	Wiley (Webatuck) Shelter
NY 3	9.5	152.3	Campsites in Edward R. Murrow Memorial Park–3.1 miles from Trail (fee)
NY 3	10.2	151.6	Telephone Pioneers Shelter
NY 4	17.4	144.4	Morgan Stewart Memorial Shelter
NY 5	23.2	138.6	Bailey Spring Campsites–0.4 mile on side trail
NY 6	26.4	135.4	RPH Shelter
NY 6	33.3	128.5	Fahnestock State Park campsites–1.0 mile NE of Trail
NY 7	36.9	124.9	Dennytown Road group campsites
NY 9	49.3	112.5	Hemlock Springs Campsite
NY 10	57.3	104.5	West Mountain Shelter–0.6 mile on side trail
NY 10	60.6	101.2	William Brien Memorial Shelter
NY 11	65.9	95.9	Fingerboard Shelter
NY 12	80.2	81.6	Wildcat Shelter
NJ 1	92.2	69.6	Wawayanda Shelter
NJ 2	105.2	56.6	Pochuck Mountain Shelter
NJ 3	117.6	44.2	High Point Shelter
NJ 4	121.8	40.0	Rutherford Shelter–0.4 mile on side trail
NJ 4	124.8	37.0	Mashipacong Shelter
NJ 4	130.5	31.3	Gren Anderson Shelter–0.3 mile on side trail
NJ 5	137.3	24.5	Brink Road Shelter–0.2 mile on side trail
NJ 6	157.2	4.6	Campsite No. 2 (no water)
NJ 6	158.8	3.0	Campsite No.1–0.5 mile on side trail (no water)

In addition, thru-hikers passing through the Delaware Water Gap National Recreation Area (parts of New Jersey Sections Five and Six) may camp along the Trail, provided they choose a site that is at least 0.5 mile from developed access roads or the boundaries of the national recreation area. Campsites must be no more than 100 feet from the Trail. Additional information is provided under "Shelters and Campsites" in New Jersey Sections Five and Six.

Shelters are generally three-sided, with open fronts. They may be fitted with bunks or have a wooden floor serving as a sleeping platform. Water, a privy, a fireplace, and, in some cases, a table and benches are usually nearby. Hikers should bring their own sleeping equipment, cooking utensils, and a stove.

Shelters along the Trail are provided primarily for the long-distance hiker who may have no other shelter. People planning overnight hikes should carry tents. This is good insurance, since the Trail is heavily used, and shelters are usually crowded during the summer. Organizations should keep their groups small (eight to ten people, including leaders), carry tents, and not monopolize the shelters. Although shelter use is on a first-come, first-served basis, please cooperate, and consider the needs of others.

If a shelter has a register, please sign it.

Shelters are for overnight stays only, and, except for bad weather, injury, or other emergency, are not intended for more than a one- or two-night duration. Hunters, fishermen, and other nonhikers should not use the shelters as bases of operation.

Use facilities with care and respect. Do not carve initials or write on shelter walls. Do not use an ax on any part of the shelter or use benches or tables as chopping blocks. The roofing material, especially if it is corrugated aluminum, is easily damaged; do not climb on it. Avoid putting excess weight or strain on wire bunks; the breaking of one wire endangers air mattresses and sleeping bags.

Be considerate of the rights of others, especially during meal times. Keep noise to a minimum between nine p.m. and seven a.m. for the sake of those attempting to sleep.

Preserve the surroundings and the ecological integrity of the site. Vandalism and carelessness mar the site's pristine nature and cause maintenance problems. Never cut live trees. Keep to trodden paths. Be conservative and careful with the environment.

Leave the shelter in good condition. Do not leave food in the shelter; this may cause damage by animals. Remove unburned trash from the fireplace, including aluminum foil, and pack out food and refuse.

Campfires

Because of the danger of forest fires, open fires on the ground are prohibited along the Trail in New York and New Jersey (except in fireplaces provided at designated campsites). Carry a portable camp stove, and use it as a substitute for an open fire.

No matter how many people use a fire, all share in responsibility for it. Be especially alert for sparks blowing from fires during high winds.

Use wood economically. Use dead or downed wood only, even if this requires searching some distance away. Many campsites have suffered visible deterioration from hikers cutting wood from trees near the site. The effective cooking fire is small. If you use wood stored in a shelter, replenish the supply.

Upon leaving the campsite, even temporarily, ensure that your fire—to the last spark—is out. Douse it with water, and overturn the ashes until all underlying coals have been thoroughly extinguished.

Conn. 341 (Kent) to Hoyt Road
Connecticut Section Six
11.5 Miles

Brief Description of Section

This section traverses the ridge of the Schaghticoke and Algo mountains, which provide numerous views of the valley below. It includes a section that follows the gorge of the Housatonic River below Bulls Bridge (one of two remaining covered bridges in Connecticut) and crosses the Ten Mile River on a 120-foot bridge.

On the ridge of Schaghticoke Mountain, the Trail passes through the Schaghticoke Indian Reservation. The tribe's original area was much larger, extending to and including the confluence of the Housatonic and Ten Mile rivers. This was the last major Indian stronghold in Connecticut; Indian settlements at the confluence may have reached back into prehistory. In 1730, 100 Indian families lived at the "divided-broad-river-place." The valley of the Ten Mile was the natural highway to the Housatonic Valley, and Indians entering there spread throughout Connecticut.

In 1994, a relocation took the Trail, from the ridge of Schaghticoke Mountain to the Bulls Bridge parking area, off paved roads and onto a protected Trail corridor. The relocated Trail descends Schaghticoke Mountain by a series of switchbacks, offers some beautiful views, and eliminates about two miles of road walking. The Trail in this section now follows paved roads for only about half a mile.

Bulls Bridge, a short distance east of the parking area on Bulls Bridge Road (which becomes Dogtail Corners Road in New York and was once a direct route between Hartford, Connecticut, and Poughkeepsie, New York), was named after an early settler who had an inn (near the present location of the Bulls Bridge Inn) that often catered to George Washington, among others. Across the road from the parking area is a Northeast Utilities dam built in 1902—worth a visit when the water is high.

Just below the gorge on the other side of the river are the remains of an old blast furnace. Kent was second to Salisbury, Connecticut, in the eighteenth century as a source of high-quality iron ore.

The Trail crosses the Ten Mile River on the Ned Anderson Memorial Bridge, built in 1983. Ned Anderson was a farmer from Sherman who designed, built, and, for 20 years, maintained the original Trail in Connecticut. It was then a project of the Connecticut Forest and Park Association (1929-1949). Interestingly enough, the Trail did not enter the town of Sherman until 1984, because before then the only way to cross the Ten Mile River was by a highway bridge in New York.

In this section, the Trail crosses the Connecticut-New York boundary three times, with the result that part of the A.T. route over Schaghticoke Mountain is in New York. This portion of the relocated Trail was designed and built by the New York-New Jersey Trail Conference; however, the entire section is maintained by the Connecticut Chapter of the Appalachian Mountain Club. The first crossing of the state line (on Schaghticoke Mountain, 4.3 miles from the northern end of the section), is marked by a sign. The third crossing is at the southern end of the section. The second crossing of the state line, on the eastern ridge of Schaghticoke Mountain, is not marked.

Road Approaches

Both the northern and southern ends of this section are accessible by vehicle. At the northern end of the section, the Trail crosses Conn. 341, 0.2 mile west of its intersection with Schaghticoke Road. Parking is available at the intersection, but overnight parking is not recommended. At the southern end, the Trail crosses Hoyt Road at the New York-Connecticut line, 0.3 mile south of the road's intersection with N.Y. 55. Parking for one or two cars is available near the Trail crossing. Road access is also available at Bulls Bridge Road. A parking area is just west of Bulls Bridge, 3.9 miles from the southern end of the section.

Public Transportation

At the northern end of the section, bus service to New York City and to Massachusetts via Bonanza Lines, (800) 556-3815, is available in Kent, Connecticut, 0.8 mile east of the Trail crossing on Conn. 341. At the southern end, rail service to New York City (Grand Central Terminal), via the Metro-North Commuter Railroad, (212) 532-4900 or (800) 638-7646, is available at the Harlem Valley-Wingdale station, 3.9 miles west of the Trail crossing of Hoyt Road.

Maps

For route navigation, refer to Map One with this guide. For area detail, refer to the following USGS 7½-minute topographic quadrangles: Kent, Connecticut; Dover Plains, New York-Connecticut.

Shelters and Campsites

This section has one shelter:

Mt. Algo Lean-to: 0.3 mile from northern end of section; 11.2 miles from southern end of section; 200 feet from the A.T. on side trail; water available.

Next shelter: north 7.6 miles (Stewart Hollow Brook Lean-to); south 12.4 miles [Wiley (Webatuck) Shelter].

Rattlesnake Den Camping Area: 3.2 miles from northern end of section; 8.3 miles from southern end of section; on blue-blazed side trail; water and privy available.

Ten Mile River Camping Area: 8.5 miles from northern end of section; 3.0 miles from southern end of section; water available from river; separate area provided for group camping; no other facilities are available.

Supplies and Services

At the northern end of the section, meals, groceries, and a post office (ZIP Code 06757) are available in Kent, 0.8 mile east of the Trail crossing of Conn. 341. At the southern end, meals and a post office (ZIP Code 12594) are available in Wingdale, 3.3 miles west of the Trail crossing of Hoyt Road. (Follow Hoyt Road north for 0.3 mile, continue west on N.Y. 55 for another 2.5 miles, turn right, and continue 0.5 mile to Wingdale.) Light meals also may be available on N.Y. 55, both 1.7 and 2.2 miles west of the Trail crossing of Hoyt Road.

In addition, a convenience store (with snacks and a limited selection of groceries) is 0.3 mile east of the Trail at Bulls Bridge, 3.9 miles from the southern end of the section (from the parking area, proceed east, and cross Bulls Bridge, then turn right on U.S. 7 for 0.1 mile).

Public Accommodations

Lodging is available in Kent, 0.8 mile east of the northern end of the section. A motel is on N.Y. 55, 4.5 miles west of the southern end of the section.

Trail Description, North to South

Miles   **Data**

0.0   From Conn. 341, ascend into woods.
0.1   Turn right on woods road for 75 feet, then turn left, and reenter woods, ascending gradually.
0.3   Blue-blazed side trail to right leads 200 feet to **Mt. Algo Lean-to** and water.
0.9   Reach height of land on Mt. Algo, and begin descent.
1.3   Cross Thayer Brook, and begin to ascend.
2.1   Reach crest of ridge on Schaghticoke Mountain, and begin steady descent.
2.4   Reach large rock, with views to south, then continue to descend.
2.9   Reach viewpoint looking up the Housatonic Valley toward Kent. Trail continues along east side of Schaghticoke Mountain, with views of Housatonic Valley and U.S. 7 below.
3.2   Descend into Rattlesnake Den, a ravine with large hemlocks and jumbled boulders. Cross brook, a reliable source of water, and ascend gradually. Just beyond brook cross-

ing, blue-blazed side trail to the right leads to **Rattlesnake Den Camping Area.**

3.4   Reach open ledge, with good views.

3.5   Descend into Dry Gulch, another rocky ravine, then ascend steeply out of Dry Gulch, and continue along east slope of Schaghticoke Mountain.

3.8   After ascent, reach Indian Rocks, a fine outlook to the east, on property of Schaghticoke Indian Reservation.

3.9   Trail comes out on open ledges, with impressive views to south and east.

4.1   Cross stream.

4.3   Note sign on tree to left of Trail, placed by Connecticut Chapter of the Appalachian Mountain Club. In another 50 feet, sign marking actual New York-Connecticut boundary is on right side of Trail. One hundred fifty feet beyond sign, pass green signboard erected by the New York-New Jersey Trail Conference, to left of Trail.

4.5   Turn left, leaving former Trail route, and begin 1994 relocation onto a newly acquired Trail corridor.

4.7   Cross stream, outlet of swamp to left of Trail.

4.9   After slight descent, cross small stream, and begin steady ascent.

5.0   Reach viewpoint from open rocks, and turn left.

5.1   At crest of rise, reach limited viewpoint to right over Ellis Pond, and begin to descend. In another 200 feet, reach second viewpoint, with slightly broader view, and continue steady descent.

5.2   Reach low point, and begin to ascend.

5.4   Pass just west of the summit of Schaghticoke Mountain (1,331 feet), and descend gradually along crest of ridge.

5.6   Reach viewpoint to southwest from open rocks. Trail turns sharply left and continues to descend.

5.7   Turn left, and begin to follow along edge of ridge.

6.1   Bear right, cross gully, pass old stone fireplace to the right, and begin steady descent of Schaghticoke Mountain on switchbacks.

6.3   Turn left, and continue along edge of ridge, with views to right when no leaves are on trees.

6.4   Descend stone steps, then turn right, and descend more steeply on short switchbacks.

6.5   Turn right, and continue to descend more gradually on long switchback to south.

6.6   Turn left at large rocks, then turn left again, and continue on long switchback to north.

6.8   Bear right, and cross stream, entering hemlock grove.

7.0   Cross stone wall, and, in 200 feet, cross stream.

7.1   Cross another stone wall, and begin to parallel stream to left. In another 300 feet, turn left, and immediately reach paved Schaghticoke Road. Turn right, and follow road.

7.4   Turn left onto paved Bulls Bridge Road.

7.6   Just before concrete bridge over a channel of the Housatonic River, turn right, go through hikers' parking area, and continue on old woods road. (Straight ahead, Bulls Bridge Road leads in about 700 feet to the historic Bulls Bridge, a covered bridge over the main channel of the Housatonic River that still carries automobile traffic.)

7.9   Bear left, leaving road, and follow trail along west bank of Housatonic River.

8.4   Pass through gap in stone wall, cross under powerline with view of Ten Mile Hill ahead, then cross small brook.

8.5   Cross Ten Mile River on Ned Anderson Memorial Bridge, named in memory of man who laid out original route of A.T. in Connecticut and maintained it for 20 years. Just before bridge, blue-blazed side trail to right leads to group camping area. The **Ten Mile River Camping Area** (for hikers not in groups) is in field immediately south of bridge. Turn right, and continue along south bank of Ten Mile River.

8.9   Turn left, and begin ascent.

9.0   Cross dirt road, with private property to right.

9.2   Turn right onto woods road, pass intermittent spring to right of Trail, and continue to ascend on footpath.

9.3   Turn left onto woods road.

9.5   Turn right, leaving woods road.

9.7   Reach top of Ten Mile Hill (1,000 feet), with limited views, and begin gradual descent.

10.5 Trail levels off.

10.8 Cross paved Conn. 55, and follow edge of field.

11.0 Cross brook, a reliable water source.

11.2 Cross end of field, and reenter woods.

11.5   Cross end of small field, and reach Hoyt Road at the Connecticut-New York state line (end of section). To continue, turn right on road (see New York Section Two).

Trail Description, South to North

Miles   **Data**

0.0   From Hoyt Road, cross end of small field, and enter woods.
0.1   Reach top of ridge.
0.3   Cross end of field, and reenter woods.
0.5   Cross brook, a reliable water source, then follow along edge of field.
0.7   Cross paved Conn. 55.
1.0   Begin to ascend.
1.8   Reach top of Ten Mile Hill (1,000 feet), with limited views, and begin gradual descent.
2.0   Turn left onto woods road, and continue to descend.
2.2   Turn right, leaving woods road.
2.3   Pass intermittent spring to left of Trail, briefly follow woods road, turn left, and continue to descend.
2.5   Cross dirt road, with private property to left.
2.6   Reach bank of Ten Mile River. Turn right, and continue along river.
3.0   Reach Ned Anderson Memorial Bridge. **Ten Mile River Camping Area** is in field south of bridge. Bridge is named in memory of the man who laid out original route of A.T. in Connecticut and maintained it for 20 years. Cross bridge, and continue along west bank of Housatonic River. Blue-blazed side trail to left, immediately after crossing bridge, leads to group camping area.
3.1   Cross small brook, then cross under powerline, with view of Ten Mile Hill looking back on Trail.
3.6   Continue straight ahead on dirt road.
3.9   Pass through hikers' parking area, and turn left onto paved Bulls Bridge Road. (To right, road leads in about 700 feet to the historic Bulls Bridge, a covered bridge over the Housatonic River that still carries automobile traffic.)

4.1   Turn right onto paved Schaghticoke Road.

4.4   Turn left, leaving road, and enter woods. Immediately, turn right, and begin to parallel stream and road. In another 300 feet, cross a stone wall, bear left, and begin to climb Schaghticoke Mountain.

4.5   Cross stone wall, and enter hemlock grove. In another 200 feet, cross stream, and ascend more steeply.

4.7   Cross stream, bear left, and follow long switchback to south.

4.8   Turn right at large rocks, then turn right again, and continue on long switchback to north.

5.0   Bear left, and ascend more steeply on short switchbacks and stone steps.

5.1   Turn left, and continue along ridge, on switchback to south, with views to the left when no leaves are on the trees.

5.2   Turn right, away from ridge, and continue to ascend on switchbacks.

5.4   With old stone fireplace to the left, bear right, cross gully, then bear left. Trail levels off.

5.6   Reach crest of rise, and descend slightly.

5.8   Turn right, away from edge of ridge, and resume ascent.

5.9   Reach viewpoint to southwest from open rocks. Trail turns sharply right and ascends gradually along crest of ridge.

6.1   Pass just west of the summit of Schaghticoke Mountain (1,331 feet), and descend gradually.

6.3   Reach low point, and begin to ascend.

6.4   Near top of climb, reach limited viewpoint to left over Ellis Pond and another lake. In another 200 feet, reach second viewpoint at crest of rise, and begin to descend.

6.5   Reach viewpoint from open rocks, and turn right.

6.6   Cross small stream, ascend slightly, descend briefly, and then level off.

6.8   Cross wider stream, outlet of swamp to right of Trail.

7.0   Turn right onto old Trail route (end of 1994 relocation).

7.2   Pass green signboard erected by New York-New Jersey Trail Conference to right of Trail. In another 150 feet, sign marking actual New York-Connecticut boundary is on left side of Trail.

7.4   Cross stream.

7.6   After left turn, reach beautiful viewpoint to the east from ledges, with impressive views of the Housatonic Valley and U.S. 7 below.

7.7   After ascent, reach Indian Rocks, a fine viewpoint to the east on the property of Schaghticoke Indian Reservation. Continue along east side of the mountain.

8.0   Descend into Dry Gulch, a narrow, rocky ravine. Then, ascend steeply out of Dry Gulch onto ridge.

8.1   Reach open ledge, with good views.

8.3   Descend into Rattlesnake Den, a ravine with large hemlocks and jumbled boulders. Cross brook, a reliable water source. Just before brook, blue-blazed side trail to the left leads to the **Rattlesnake Den Camping Area**. Ascend steeply, then continue along east side of ridge, with views to east.

8.6   Reach viewpoint over Housatonic Valley toward Kent.

9.1   After ascent, reach large rock, with views to south, then continue ascent.

9.4   Reach height of land, and begin descent off Schaghticoke Mountain.

10.2   Cross Thayer Brook, and ascend.

10.6   Reach height of land on Mt. Algo, and begin to descend.

11.2   Blue-blazed side trail to left leads 200 feet to **Mt. Algo Lean-to** and water.

11.4   Turn right on woods road for 75 feet, turn left, and continue to descend.

11.5   Reach paved Conn. 341 (end of section). To continue, cross highway, and enter pasture on opposite side of highway. The description of A.T. continues in the *Appalachian Trail Guide to Massachusetts-Connecticut.*

Hoyt Road to N.Y. 22 (Pawling)
New York Section Two
7.1 Miles

Brief Description of Section

This section is mostly woodland trails. The woods are second growth, ranging from scrubby to mature. Several fine groves of hemlocks can be observed along the way, as well as good stands of mixed hardwoods along the Hammersly Ridge. Along the ridge, the Trail passes through several marshy areas. At a few points, one is able to glimpse the rolling, southern Dutchess County countryside. The elevation at Hoyt Road is 420 feet, and, at N.Y. 22, it is 450 feet. The highest point is on the Hammersly Ridge in the Pawling Nature Reserve, with an elevation of 1,053 feet.

This area was farmed extensively during Revolutionary times, but much of the land has reverted to forest. A large portion has been incorporated into sizeable private estates, as well as the thousand-acre Pawling Nature Reserve, owned by The Nature Conservancy. Evidence of the past can be observed in the crumbling stone walls, foundations, and dams. Notice the traces of abandoned orchards, fields, and roads visible along the Trail.

Road Approaches

Both the northern and southern ends of this section are accessible by vehicle. At the northern end, the Trail crosses Hoyt Road at the New York-Connecticut line, 0.3 mile south of the road's intersection with N.Y. 55. Parking is available for one or two cars near the Trail crossing. At the southern end, the Trail crosses N.Y. 22, 1.1 miles north of Corbin Road and 2.4 miles north of the center of the village of Pawling. A designated parking area is located just north of the Trail crossing.

Road access is also available at Duell Hollow Road, which crosses the Trail 1.0 mile from the northern end of the section. Parking is available just south of the Trail crossing, near an old cemetery.

Public Transportation

Rail service to New York City (Grand Central Terminal) via the Metro-North Commuter Railroad, (212) 532-4900 or (800) 638-7646, is available at Pawling, 2.4 miles south of the Trail crossing of N.Y. 22 at the southern end of the section, and at the Harlem Valley-Wingdale station, 3.9 miles west of the Trail crossing of Hoyt Road at the northern end of the section. On weekends and holidays, Metro-North provides rail service at the Appalachian Trail station, just west of the Trail crossing of N.Y. 22 at the southern end of the section.

Limited bus service to Pawling and Poughkeepsie, via Loops 2b and 4a of the Dutchess County Loop Bus System, (914) 485-4690, is available at the Trail crossing of N.Y. 22 at the southern end of the section.

Maps

For route navigation, refer to Map One with this guide. For area detail, refer to the following USGS 7½-minute topographic quadrangles: Dover Plains, New York-Connecticut; Pawling, New York-Connecticut. Another reference is the map of Pawling Nature Reserve available from the Lower Hudson Chapter of The Nature Conservancy, 233 Katonah Avenue, Katonah, N.Y. 10536, (914) 232-9431.

Shelters and Campsites

This section has one shelter:

Wiley (Webatuck) Shelter: Built in 1940, with assistance from William O. Wiley of the Tramp and Trail Club of New York, on property of Camp Siwanoy, Westchester-Putnam Council, Boy Scouts of America; 1.2 miles from northern end of section; 5.9 miles from southern end of section; accommodates 6; water available from cistern on Trail 0.1 mile north of the shelter.

Next shelter: north 12.4 miles (Mt. Algo Lean-to); south 9.0 miles (Telephone Pioneers Shelter).

Supplies and Services

At the northern end of the section, meals and a post office (ZIP Code 12594) are available in Wingdale, 3.3 miles west of the Trail crossing of Hoyt Road. (Follow Hoyt Road north for 0.3 mile, then continue west on N.Y. 55 for another 2.5 miles, turn right, and continue 0.5 mile to Wingdale.) Light meals also may be available on N.Y. 55, both 1.7 and 2.2 miles west of the Trail crossing of Hoyt Road.

At the southern end of the section, a grocery store is located on N.Y. 22, 0.6 mile south of the Trail crossing. Groceries, meals, a post office (ZIP Code 12564), a laundromat, and other supplies and services are available in Pawling, 2.4 miles south of the Trail crossing of N.Y. 22. (Proceed south on N.Y. 22 for 1.2 miles, turn right onto Corbin Road for 0.4 mile, then turn left, and continue on Charles Colman Boulevard 0.8 mile to the center of Pawling.) The post office is on Broad Street, just west of the center of town. A supermarket (open seven days a week) is on East Main Street, 0.2 mile east of the intersection of Charles Colman Boulevard and East Main Street.

Public Accommodations

The southern end of the section has a motel 2.6 miles north of the Trail crossing. The motel also can be reached from the northern end of the section by following N.Y. 55, 4.5 miles to the west and south.

Trail Description, North to South

Miles	Data
0.0	From Connecticut-New York state line, proceed north on Hoyt Road.
0.1	Turn left, and ascend through woods.
0.2	Follow posts across overgrown field, turn right onto woods road, then turn left, and enter field. Bear right, and follow along right edge of field.
0.3	Reenter woods.
0.7	Cross wooden bridge over Duell Hollow Brook.

1.0   Reach paved Duell Hollow Road. Cross road diagonally to left, and reenter woods; soon, begin to ascend.

1.1   Pass cistern, a water source.

1.2   Pass through gap in stone wall, then turn left, pass in front of **Wiley (Webatuck) Shelter**, and recross stone wall.

1.3   Cross dirt logging road.

1.4   Trail levels off, then begins to descend.

1.6   Cross dirt Leather Hill Road diagonally to right, then begin to ascend.

1.7   Pass through gap in stone wall. In another 300 feet, cross stream.

1.9   Turn left onto old woods road.

2.1   Cross cleared strip of land (telephone cable). In another 90 feet, cross stone wall.

2.3   Cross stream.

2.4   Turn right onto grassy road that curves to left and passes Gate of Heaven Cemetery on right.

2.6   Turn right, and, in 65 feet, cross gravel road. Continue across overgrown field.

2.7   Turn right, and reenter woods.

3.0   Pass through gap in stone wall.

3.1   Pass through gap in stone wall and fence. In another 250 feet, cross stream on rocks.

3.3   Cross stream on logs.

3.5   Enter Pawling Nature Reserve.

3.6   Yellow-blazed trail begins to left and leads to north entrance of Pawling Nature Reserve on Quaker Lake Road (Duell Hollow Road). In another 200 feet, cross seasonal stream, and ascend steeply, then cross stone wall, and descend gradually.

3.8   Pass stone wall to left of Trail.

4.4   Cross swampy area on logs.

4.5   Turn right as red-blazed trail goes off to left. In another 125 feet, green-blazed trail goes off to right.

4.6   Begin crossing of swampy area on long stretch of puncheon. Red-blazed trail soon begins to right.

4.9   Cross stream. In another 200 feet, turn right as yellow-blazed trail continues straight ahead. (Yellow-blazed trail leads to main entrance of Pawling Nature Reserve on

Quaker Lake Road.) Soon, pass through mountain-laurel thicket.

5.2	Cross stream.
5.3	Pass swamp to right of Trail.
5.4	Cross red-blazed trail.
5.6	Begin to descend from top of ridge.
6.1	Continue to descend through field.
6.2	Reenter woods, soon crossing brook. In another 75 feet, to right of Trail, please sign register installed by Pawling Nature Reserve.
6.6	Cross swampy area on rocks, and reach paved Hurds Corners Road. Turn left, and follow road.
6.9	Turn right, pass through gap in barbed-wire fence, and follow posts along field.
7.1	Reach N.Y. 22 (end of section). To continue, cross road, and proceed south on N.Y. 22 (see New York Section Three).

Trail Description, South to North

Miles   **Data**

0.0	From east side of N.Y. 22, proceed east, following posts along field.
0.2	Turn left onto paved Hurds Corners Road.
0.5	Turn right, to enter woods and Pawling Nature Reserve. Cross swampy area on rocks.
0.8	Please sign register to left of Trail, installed by Pawling Nature Reserve. In another 75 feet, cross brook, then pass through field, ascending gradually.
1.0	Bear left, and reenter woods. Soon cross old stone wall.
1.3	Turn right before reaching gap in stone wall.
1.5	Reach top of ridge, and begin to descend.
1.7	Cross red-blazed trail.
1.8	Pass swamp to left of Trail.
1.9	Cross stream.
2.0	Enter mountain-laurel thicket.
2.2	Turn left onto level trail as yellow-blazed trail comes in from right. (Yellow-blazed trail leads to main entrance of

Pawling Nature Reserve on Quaker Lake Road.) In another 200 feet, cross stream.

2.4   Begin crossing of swampy area on long stretch of puncheon.

2.5   Red-blazed trail begins to left.

2.6   Continue straight ahead as green-blazed trail begins on left. In another 125 feet, turn left as red-blazed trail goes off to right.

2.7   Cross swampy area on logs.

3.3   Pass stone wall to left of Trail.

3.5   Cross stone wall, and descend steeply to cross seasonal stream, then ascend. In another 200 feet, yellow-blazed trail begins to right and leads to north entrance of Pawling Nature Reserve on Quaker Lake Road (Duell Hollow Road).

3.6   Leave Pawling Nature Reserve.

3.8   Bear left at fork. In another 125 feet, cross stream on logs.

4.0   Cross stream on rocks. In another 250 feet, pass through gap in fence and stone wall.

4.1   Pass through gap in stone wall.

4.4   Reach overgrown field, and turn left.

4.5   Cross gravel road. In another 65 feet, turn right onto grassy road.

4.7   With Gate of Heaven Cemetery to left, turn right, then immediately bear left on trail, and reenter woods.

4.8   Cross stream.

5.0   Cross stone wall. In another 90 feet, cross cleared strip of land (telephone cable).

5.1   Cross stone wall, and descend, soon following old woods road.

5.2   Turn right, and continue to descend on footpath.

5.3   Cross stream. In another 300 feet, pass through gap in stone wall.

5.5   Cross dirt Leather Hill Road diagonally to right, then begin to ascend.

5.7   Begin steady descent.

5.8   Cross dirt logging road.

5.9   Pass through gap in stone wall, then pass in front of **Wiley (Webatuck) Shelter**, turn right, and recross stone wall.

6.0   Pass cistern, a water source.

6.1   Reach paved Duell Hollow Road. Cross road diagonally
      to left, and reenter woods.
6.4   Cross wooden bridge over Duell Hollow Brook.
6.8   Emerge onto field. Follow along left edge of field, then
      turn left, immediately bear right, and descend on woods
      road.
6.9   Turn left, and follow posts across overgrown field, then
      descend through woods.
7.0   Reach paved Hoyt Road. Turn right, and follow road.
7.1   Reach New York-Connecticut state line (end of section).
      To continue, turn left, and cross end of small field (see
      Connecticut Section Six).

N.Y. 22 (Pawling) to N.Y. 55 (Poughquag)
New York Section Three
7.0 Miles

Brief Description of Section

The northern part of this section climbs Corbin Hill, proceeds through open fields, and then steeply climbs West Mountain to a beautiful viewpoint over the countryside to the east. The southern part of the section was once the property of the United Nuclear Corporation.

The Trail does not pass close to the site once used by the United Nuclear Corporation for nuclear-fuel testing and research. The corporation ceased operating in December 1972 after two non-nuclear explosions released plutonium dust into the surrounding environment. Following site decontamination, the Nuclear Regulatory Commission and the New York State Department of Environmental Conservation cleared the site for "unrestricted use." Subsequent extensive testing found elevated levels of radiation in two of the buildings. The National Park Service directed a complete clean-up, removing all buildings and restoring the area. However, public access to the lake and the site of the former buildings is prohibited at this time.

The New York-New Jersey Trail Conference and the Dutchess-Putnam A.T. Local Management Committee endorse the use of the footpath through this property, because tests have not disclosed any unusual levels of radiation along the Trail route. (The Trail route comes no closer than a quarter-mile to the United Nuclear site.) It is a beautiful area, and we hope that you will enjoy walking through it. However, if you prefer not to walk through these woods, a roadwalk is maintained as a blue-blazed alternate trail. Please remember to stay to the side of the road and use caution when road-walking.

Road Approaches

Both the northern and southern ends of this section are accessible by vehicle. The northern end of the section is on N.Y. 22, 1.1 miles north of Corbin Road and 2.4 miles north of the center of the village of Pawling. A designated parking area is located just north of the Trail crossing. The southern end of the section is on N.Y. 55, about 1.4 miles southeast of its intersection with Pleasant Ridge Road and 1.5 miles southeast of its intersection with N.Y. 216. A designated parking area is located just west of the Trail crossing.

Road access is also available at County 20 (West Dover Road), which crosses the Trail 2.4 miles from the northern end of the section.

Public Transportation

Rail service to New York City (Grand Central Terminal) via the Metro-North Commuter Railroad, (212) 532-4900 or (800) 638-7646, is available at Pawling, 2.4 miles south of the Trail crossing of N.Y. 22 at the northern end of the section. Pawling may also be reached by proceeding south on County 20 (West Dover Road), which intersects the Trail 2.4 miles from the northern end of the section. Continue south on County 20 for 2.9 miles to the center of Pawling. (After 2.1 miles, at intersection with Corbin Road and Lakeside Drive, the road name changes to Charles Colman Boulevard.)

On weekends and holidays, Metro-North provides rail service at the Appalachian Trail station, just west of the Trail crossing of N.Y. 22 at the northern end of the section.

Limited bus service to Pawling and Poughkeepsie, via Loops 2b and 4a of the Dutchess County Loop Bus System, (914) 485-4690, is available at both the Trail crossing of N.Y. 22 at the northern end of the section and the Trail crossing of N.Y. 55 at the southern end of the section.

Maps

For route navigation, refer to Map One with this guide. For area detail, refer to the following USGS 7½-minute topographic quadrangles: Pawling, New York-Connecticut; Poughquag, New York.

Shelters and Campsites

This section has one shelter:

Telephone Pioneers Shelter: Built in 1988, with assistance from the White Plains Council of the Telephone Pioneers of America; 3.1 miles from northern end of section; 3.9 miles from southern end of section; 0.1 mile from A.T. on side trail; accommodates 6; water from stream crossed by side trail to shelter; privy 200 feet from shelter on side trail.

Next shelter: north 9.0 miles [Wiley (Webatuck) Shelter]; south 7.2 miles (Morgan Stewart Memorial Shelter).

One public campground is also near the Trail:

Edward R. Murrow Memorial Park: Named in memory of Edward R. Morrow, a pioneer of American broadcast journalism, who was a resident of Pawling at the time of his death in 1965. Operated by Pawling Recreation Department, (914) 855-1131; at junction of Lakeside Drive and Old N.Y. 55, 3.1 miles from the Trail crossing of County 20 (West Dover Road), which is 2.4 miles from the northern end of the section and 4.6 miles from the southern end of section. Follow County 20 south for 2.1 miles, then turn right onto Lakeside Drive for 1.0 mile; open year-round; nominal fee charged; swimming, hot showers, and snack bar available during season (Memorial Day to Labor Day); picnic shelters with fireplaces also available.

Supplies and Services

The northern end of the section has a grocery store on N.Y. 22, 0.6 mile south of the Trail crossing. Groceries, meals, a post office (ZIP Code 12564), a laundromat, and other supplies and services are available in Pawling, 2.4 miles south of the Trail crossing of N.Y. 22. (Proceed south on N.Y. 22 for 1.2 miles, turn right onto Corbin Road for 0.4 mile, then turn left, and continue on Charles Colman Boulevard 0.8 mile to the center of Pawling.) The post office is on Broad Street, just west of the center of town. A supermarket (open seven days a week) is on East Main Street, 0.2 mile east of the intersection of Charles Colman Boulevard and East Main Street. Pawling also may be reached by proceeding south on County 20

(West Dover Road), which intersects the Trail 2.4 miles from the northern end of the section. Continue south on County 20 for 2.9 miles to the center of Pawling (after 2.1 miles, at intersection with Corbin Road and Lakeside Drive, the road name changes to Charles Colman Boulevard).

The southern end of the section has a large grocery store (open seven days a week) at the intersection of N.Y. 55 and N.Y. 216, 1.5 miles northwest of the Trail crossing of N.Y. 55. A limited selection of groceries and light meals are available just west of the intersection of N.Y. 216 and County 7, 2.0 miles from the end of the section (proceed west on N.Y. 55 for 1.5 miles, turn left onto N.Y. 216 for 0.4 mile, then turn right onto County 7). Meals and a post office (ZIP Code 12570) are available in Poughquag, on N.Y. 55, 3.1 miles west of the end of the section.

Public Accommodations

A motel is located on N.Y. 22, 2.6 miles north of the northern end of the section. A motel is also located on N.Y. 55, 2.6 miles west of the southern end of the section.

Trail Description, North to South

Miles   **Data**

0.0   From the end of New York Section Two, proceed south on N.Y. 22.
0.1   Turn right onto dirt road, cross railroad tracks at the Appalachian Trail railroad station, go around gate, and follow road alongside field.
0.4   Cross marshy area on puncheon, cross wooden bridge over Swamp River, turn right, and begin steady ascent of Corbin Hill.
0.9   Pass through gap in stone wall.
1.1   Pass through large gap in another stone wall.
1.5   Reach top of hill. Trail levels off.
1.6   Emerge onto open field. Turn left, and continue along left side of field.

1.7   Cross barbed-wire fence on stile, turn left, and follow posts across field.

1.9   Skirt edge of field on puncheon and bridges in marshy area. The fence around the field may be electrified; use care.

2.4   Descend stone steps, pass huge white oak to right of Trail, and cross paved County 20 (West Dover Road). On opposite side of road, turn right, and follow posts.

2.5   Turn left, and descend slightly to cross wet area. Continue to follow posts through open fields.

2.6   Pass through gap in stone wall, ascend over rocks, then pass old farm machinery.

2.7   Cross stream, and turn right, beginning steep ascent of West Mountain and paralleling stream on right.

2.8   Trail levels off, turns away from stream, and soon resumes steep ascent.

3.1   Side trail on left leads 0.1 mile to **Telephone Pioneers Shelter** (water usually available from stream crossed by side trail to shelter).

3.2   Trail begins to level off.

3.3   Side trail to right leads 100 feet to rocky ledge with beautiful views over farmlands below to east.

3.4   Reach summit of West Mountain, with good northern views, and begin gradual descent.

3.8   Pass swamp to right of Trail.

3.9   Cross dirt Penny Road (not passable by car). (Former A.T. route, now blue-blazed alternate trail, turns right onto Penny Road.)

4.1   After descent, cross brook, then cross swampy area on puncheon.

4.3   Cross stone wall, descend briefly, then ascend gradually.

4.5   Pass through gap in stone wall, and descend steeply.

4.8   Briefly follow old road that bisects rocky valley.

5.2   Pass swampy area to left of Trail, then ascend steeply.

6.1   Cross dry area between two swamps.

6.6   Go through narrow passage between rocks, and pass jumbled boulders to right.

6.7   Blue-blazed side trail to right leads to parking area on N.Y. 55.

6.9   Pass under powerlines.

7.0   Reach paved N.Y. 55 (end of section). To continue, cross road, and reenter woods (see New York Section Four).

Trail Description, South to North

Miles   **Data**

0.0   From N.Y. 55, proceed north on Trail, soon passing under powerlines.

0.3   Blue-blazed side trail to left leads to parking area on N.Y. 55.

0.4   Pass jumbled boulders to left, then go through narrow passage between rocks.

0.9   Cross dry area between two swamps.

1.8   After steep descent, pass swampy area to right of Trail.

2.2   Briefly follow old road that bisects rocky valley.

2.5   After steep ascent, pass through gap in stone wall, then descend gradually.

2.7   After brief ascent, cross stone wall.

2.9   Cross swampy area on puncheon, then cross brook, and begin to ascend.

3.1   Cross dirt Penny Road (not passable by car). (Blue-blazed alternate trail comes in from left.)

3.2   Pass swamp to left of Trail.

3.6   Reach summit of West Mountain, with good northern views, and begin to descend.

3.7   Side trail to left leads 100 feet to rocky ledge, with beautiful views over farmlands below to east.

3.8   Begin steep descent.

3.9   Side trail on right leads 0.1 mile to **Telephone Pioneers Shelter** (water usually available from stream crossed by side trail to shelter).

4.2   Trail levels off briefly, then resumes steep descent, paralleling stream to left.

4.3   Turn left, and cross stream. Trail levels off.

4.4   After passing old farm machinery, climb over rocks, then descend, pass through gap in stone wall, and follow posts through open fields.

4.5   Descend slightly to cross wet area, then turn right, and continue following posts.

4.6   Cross paved County Route 20 (West Dover Road). On opposite side of road, pass huge white oak to left of Trail, ascend stone steps, and follow posts across grassy field.

4.8   Skirt edge of field on puncheon and bridges in marshy area. Fence around field on the left may be electrified; use care. As the Trail ascends, follow posts through fields.

5.3   Near end of field, turn left, then turn right, and cross barbed-wire fence on stile. Continue along right side of field, with woods to right.

5.5   Turn right, and reenter woods; soon, begin to descend.

5.9   Pass through large gap in stone wall.

6.1   Pass through gap in another stone wall.

6.6   After making sharp left turn, cross wooden bridge over Swamp River. Continue through marshy area on puncheon, and follow dirt road alongside field.

6.9   Go around gate, cross railroad tracks at the Appalachian Trail railroad station, and reach N.Y. 22. Turn left, and continue along road.

7.0   Turn right, and cross road (end of section). To continue, follow posts along field (see New York Section Two).

N.Y. 55 (Poughquag) to
N.Y. 52 (Stormville)
New York Section Four
7.2 Miles

Brief Description of Section

This section goes over Depot Hill, with several beautiful views from rock ledges. Except for a few short stretches along roads, the Trail is on footpaths through woods. The elevation at the northern end of the section is about 470 feet, and, at the southern end, it is about 850 feet. The highest point in the section is at the summit of Mt. Egbert on Depot Hill, which is 1,329 feet.

Road Approaches

Both the northern and southern ends of this section are accessible by vehicle. The northern end is on N.Y. 55, about 1.4 miles southeast of its intersection with Pleasant Ridge Road and 1.5 miles southeast of its intersection with N.Y. 216. A designated parking area is located just west of the Trail crossing. The southern end is on N.Y. 52, 0.4 mile north of the intersection of N.Y. 52 with Leetown Road, and 2.2 miles south of Stormville (on Old N.Y. 52). A designated parking area is located just north of the Trail crossing. Road access is also available at Grape Hollow Road and Mountain Top Road at the I-84 overpass, 1.3 miles from the southern end of the section, and at Depot Hill Road, which the Trail crosses 2.2 miles from the northern end of the section. Parking is available at or near those locations.

Public Transportation

Limited bus service to Pawling and Poughkeepsie, via Loops 2b and 4a of the Dutchess County Loop Bus System, (914) 485-4690, is available at the Trail crossing of N.Y. 55 at the northern end of the section.

Maps

For route navigation, refer to Map One with this guide. For area detail, refer to the following USGS 7½-minute topographic quadrangle: Poughquag, New York.

Shelters and Campsites

This section has one shelter:

Morgan Stewart Memorial Shelter: Built in 1984 of prefabricated wood; 3.3 miles from northern end of section; 3.9 miles from southern end of section; 75 feet from the A.T. on side trail; accommodates 6; water from well on 400-foot side trail leading downhill from front of shelter; privy located 200 feet from shelter on side trail.

Next shelter: north 7.2 miles (Telephone Pioneers Shelter); south 9.0 miles (RPH Shelter).

Supplies and Services

The northern end of the section has a large grocery store (open seven days a week) at the intersection of N.Y. 55 and N.Y. 216, 1.5 miles northwest of the Trail crossing of N.Y. 55. A limited selection of groceries and light meals are available just west of the intersection of N.Y. 216 and County 7, 2.0 miles from the end of the section. (Proceed west on N.Y. 55 for 1.5 miles, turn left onto N.Y. 216 for 0.4 mile, then turn right onto County 7.) Meals and a post office (ZIP Code 12570) are available in Poughquag, on N.Y. 55, 3.1 miles west of the end of the section.

At the southern end of the section, groceries and sandwiches are available at a store (open seven days a week) 0.5 mile south of the Trail crossing of N.Y. 52. (Follow N.Y. 52 south for 0.4 mile, then turn right onto Leetown Road, and continue 0.1 mile to the store.) Groceries and light meals are also available at a store (open seven days a week) 2.0 miles south of the Trail crossing on N.Y. 52. Stormville has a post office (ZIP Code 12582) and a meat market that carries a limited selection of groceries (closed Mondays), 2.2 miles north of the Trail crossing of N.Y. 52. (Proceed north on N.Y. 52 for 1.7 miles, then turn right onto Old N.Y. 52, and continue for 0.5

mile.) Another store with a limited supply of groceries (open seven days a week) and a public telephone is 0.2 mile farther north, at the intersection of Old N.Y. 52 and N.Y. 216.

Public Accommodations

A motel is located on N.Y. 55, 2.6 miles west of the northern end of the section.

Trail Description, North to South

Miles	Data
0.0	From N.Y. 55, proceed south on Trail.
0.3	Reach paved Old N.Y. 55. (Blue-blazed alternate trail comes in from right and rejoins Trail.) Cross road, descend wooden steps, and cross muddy area on rocks.
0.4	Cross wooden bridge over Whaley Lake Stream, then ascend railroad embankment. Cross railroad tracks, and descend from embankment. Cross small brook, and soon begin ascending.
0.6	Cross bed of intermittent stream, then turn right, and resume steady ascent.
0.9	Pass balanced rock to left as Trail levels off.
1.2	Resume steady ascent.
1.6	After brief descent, cross boundary of state forest (marked by yellow blazes on trees). In another 150 feet, turn right, cross stream, and soon resume gradual ascent.
1.8	Begin to descend.
1.9	Pass through narrow passage between rocks, then pass swamp to left of Trail. Continue descent.
2.1	Begin to ascend.
2.2	Cross unpaved Depot Hill Road.
2.7	Pass seasonal pond to left of Trail, then turn right, and descend through narrow ravine. In 150 feet from base of ravine, descend rock steps. Trail levels off.
2.9	Begin to ascend.
3.0	Reach rock ledge with good views to north as Trail levels off.

3.1   Descend briefly over rocks.

3.3   Side trail on left leads 75 feet to **Morgan Stewart Memo-rial Shelter**. Trail from shelter leads downhill 400 feet to a well (dependable water source).

3.4   Pass U.S. Coast and Geodetic Survey marker on rock at summit of Mt. Egbert (1,329 feet).

3.6   Reach flat rock, and turn right. In another 200 feet, emerge on ledge with good views to west and south, then begin to descend from crest of ridge, steeply in places.

3.7   Pass old stone foundation to right as Trail levels off.

3.9   Descend steeply through mountain laurel, cross brook, and ascend.

4.3   Ascend steeply, pass through cleft in rock, then descend.

4.6   Descend into hollow, turn right, then left, and ascend.

5.5   Cross hollow, with swampy area to left.

5.8   Climb stone steps up road embankment, and emerge onto paved Grape Hollow Road. Continue straight ahead on Mountain Top Road, and cross I-84 overpass.

6.0   Turn right onto unpaved Stormville Mountain Road.

6.2   At dead end of road, turn left, and ascend on footpath into woods, then descend gradually.

6.4   Emerge onto overgrown field, with portions cleared as part of an open-areas management project for improved views and natural diversity. There are wide views of the Shawangunk and Catskill mountains to the north and northwest.

6.6   Cross stone wall, and reenter woods, then descend to cross small stream.

6.7   Pass through gap in old stone wall.

7.0   Continue to descend as footpath gradually widens to grassy woods road.

7.1   Turn left, leaving woods road. (Straight ahead, blue-blazed trail follows woods road for 250 feet to parking area on N.Y. 52).

7.2   Reach paved N.Y. 52. Cross road, turn left, and continue along road for 125 feet to end of section. To continue, turn right, and reenter woods on footpath (see New York Section Five).

Trail Description, South to North

Miles	Data

0.0   Where northbound Trail reaches N.Y. 52, 0.4 mile north of Leetown Road, continue north along N.Y. 52 for 125 feet, then cross road, and reenter woods on footpath.

0.1   Turn right onto grassy woods road. (To left, blue-blazed trail follows woods road for 250 feet to parking area on N.Y. 52). Ascend gradually as road narrows to footpath.

0.5   Pass through gap in old stone wall, and descend to cross small stream.

0.6   After brief ascent, cross stone wall, and emerge onto overgrown field, with portions cleared as part of an open-areas management project for improved views and natural diversity. There are wide views of the Shawangunk and Catskill mountains to the north and northwest.

0.8   Turn right, and reenter woods, ascending gradually.

1.0   After brief descent, emerge onto dead end of unpaved Stormville Mountain Road. Turn right, and follow road.

1.2   Turn left onto paved Mountain Top Road, and continue across I-84 overpass.

1.4   Reach Grape Hollow Road. Continue straight ahead, cross guardrail, and descend stone steps down road embankment, reentering woods. Ascend gradually.

1.7   Cross hollow, with swampy area to right.

2.6   Descend into hollow, turn right, then left, and ascend.

2.9   Ascend through cleft in rock, then descend steeply.

3.3   Descend to cross brook, then ascend steeply through mountain laurel.

3.5   Pass old stone foundation to left of Trail. Soon begin ascent, steeply in places, through mountain-laurel thicket.

3.6   Reach crest of Mt. Egbert, with good views to west and south. In another 200 feet, reach flat rock, and turn left.

3.8   Pass U.S. Coast and Geodetic Survey marker on rock at summit of Mt. Egbert (1,329 feet).

3.9   Side trail on right leads 75 feet to **Morgan Stewart Memorial Shelter**. Trail from shelter leads downhill 400 feet to a well (dependable water source).

4.1   Ascend briefly over rocks.

4.2   Reach rock ledge with good views to north, and begin gradual descent.

4.3   Trail levels off.

4.4   Ascend rock steps. In another 150 feet, climb through narrow ravine, then pass seasonal pond to right of Trail.

5.0   Cross unpaved Depot Hill Road. Begin to descend, then ascend.

5.3   Pass swamp to right of Trail. Pass through narrow passage between rocks, and ascend moderately.

5.4   Begin steady, gradual descent.

5.6   Cross stream, and turn left as Trail levels off. In another 150 feet, cross boundary of state forest (marked by yellow blazes on trees). Ascend briefly, then begin steady descent.

6.0   Trail levels off.

6.3   Pass balanced rock to right, and resume steady descent.

6.6   Turn left, and cross bed of intermittent stream.

6.8   Cross small brook. Climb wooden steps up railroad embankment, cross railroad tracks, and descend from embankment. Cross wooden bridge over Whaley Lake Stream.

6.9   Cross muddy area on rocks. Ascend wooden steps, and cross paved Old N.Y. 55. (Blue-blazed alternate trail turns left onto Old N.Y. 55.)

7.2   Reach paved N.Y. 55 (end of section). To continue, cross road, and reenter woods (see New York Section Three).

N.Y. 52 (Stormville) to Taconic State Parkway
New York Section Five
4.8 Miles

Brief Description of Section

This section of the Trail traverses the multiple summits of Stormville Mountain and the western side of Hosner Mountain (not reaching the ridge itself). Good views are to the north and west over the Hudson River Valley. Elevation at N.Y. 52 is 800 feet; at the Taconic State Parkway, 540 feet. The section's highest elevation is about 1,040 feet, on Hosner Mountain.

Road Approaches

Both the northern and southern ends of this section are accessible by vehicle. The northern end is on N.Y. 52, 0.4 mile north of the intersection of N.Y. 52 with Leetown Road and 2.2 miles south of Stormville (on Old N.Y. 52). A designated parking area is located just north of the Trail crossing. The southern end is at the intersection of the Taconic State Parkway with Miller Hill Road. No parking is available at the parkway crossing, but limited parking is available at the Trail crossing of Hortontown Road, 0.4 mile to the south.

Public Transportation

Public transportation is unavailable at either end of this section.

Maps

For route navigation, refer to Map Two with this guide. For area detail, refer to the following USGS 7½-minute topographic quadrangles: Poughquag and Hopewell Junction, New York.

Shelters and Campsites

This section of the Trail has one camping area:

Bailey Spring Campsites: 1.9 miles from northern end of section; 2.9 miles from southern end of section; on 0.4-mile side trail; water available from spring; no other facilities are available.

Supplies and Services

A store (open seven days a week) at the northern end of the section, 0.5 mile south of the Trail crossing of N.Y. 52, has groceries and sandwiches. (Follow N.Y. 52 south for 0.4 mile, then turn right onto Leetown Road, and continue 0.1 mile to the store.) Groceries and light meals also are available at a store (open seven days a week) 2.0 miles south of the Trail crossing on N.Y. 52. Stormville has a post office (ZIP Code 12582) and a meat market that carries a limited supply of groceries (closed Mondays), 2.2 miles north of the Trail crossing of N.Y. 52. (Proceed north on N.Y. 52 for 1.7 miles, then turn right onto Old N.Y. 52, and continue for 0.5 mile.) Another store with a limited selection of groceries (open seven days a week) and a public telephone is 0.2 mile farther north, at the intersection of Old N.Y. 52 and N.Y. 216.

At the southern end, groceries are available in Shenandoah, on Miller Hill Road, 1.2 miles north of the intersection of Miller Hill Road with the Taconic State Parkway.

Public Accommodations

No accommodations are available in this section.

Trail Description, North to South

Miles	Data
0.0	From N.Y. 52, begin gradual ascent.
0.3	Continue ascending on switchbacks.
0.5	Reach first summit of Stormville Mountain, and begin descent.

0.8   Pass old trail to right, and begin ascent of second summit of Stormville Mountain.

1.0   Reach viewpoint to right, over the Hudson River Valley, at the second summit of Stormville Mountain. Begin to descend.

1.3   Descend more steeply on rock steps.

1.4   Trail makes sharp left turn, levels off, then descends more moderately through hemlock grove.

1.6   Cross bridge over small brook, and reach paved Hosner Mountain Road. Cross road, and begin to ascend.

1.9   Blue-blazed side trail to right leads 0.4 mile to Bailey Spring, a water source, with adjacent **campsites**. Continue along west slope of Hosner Mountain, paralleling ridge.

2.2   Pass through large hemlock grove.

2.4   To right are views north and west over the Hudson River Valley, with intersection of I-84 and the Taconic State Parkway below. Trail continues along shoulder of ridge, becoming very rocky.

2.9   Bear left, and begin to ascend, steeply in places. Blue-blazed trail to right (old A.T. route) parallels relocated Trail but runs lower on the hillside. It rejoins the A.T. in 0.5 mile and may be used to make a circuit hike.

3.1   Trail levels off and begins to run along rocky ledge, with views to right through the trees.

3.2   Reach beautiful viewpoint over Hudson Highlands, Shawangunks, and Catskills, then descend rock steps.

3.4   Blue-blazed trail (old A.T. route) rejoins from right.

3.5   Cross small brook.

3.8   Reach viewpoint to north and west from rock ledge to right of Trail. A.T. begins to descend.

4.0   Pass rock ledges and boulder outcroppings to left of Trail. In another 200 feet, pass stone wall to left.

4.6   Pass through hemlock grove.

4.7   Turn left on unpaved Rock Ledge Road that runs parallel to Taconic State Parkway.

4.8   Turn right onto Miller Hill Road, and reach Taconic State Parkway (end of section). To continue, cross parkway, and proceed west on Miller Hill Road (see New York Section Six).

Trail Description, South to North

Miles   **Data**

0.0   From Taconic State Parkway at Miller Hill Road, proceed east on Miller Hill Road for 50 feet, then turn left onto unpaved Rock Ledge Road that runs parallel to parkway.

0.1   Turn right, leaving road, and begin ascent of Hosner Mountain.

0.2   Pass through hemlock grove. Trail levels off, then resumes ascent. Continue along shoulder of ridge of Hosner Mountain, with many short ascents and descents.

0.8   Pass stone wall to right, and continue gradual ascent. In another 200 feet, pass rock ledges and boulder outcroppings to right of Trail.

1.0   Reach viewpoint to north and west from rock ledge to left of Trail.

1.3   Cross small brook.

1.4   Bear right on relocated trail. Blue-blazed trail to left (old A.T. route) parallels relocated trail but runs lower on the hillside. It rejoins the A.T. in 0.5 mile and may be used to make a circuit hike.

1.6   After climbing rock steps, reach beautiful viewpoint over Hudson Highlands, Shawangunks, and Catskills. Continue along rocky ledge, with views to left through the trees.

1.7   Begin steady descent.

1.9   Blue-blazed trail (old A.T. route) rejoins from left. A.T. levels off and becomes very rocky.

2.4   To left are views north and west over the Hudson River Valley, with intersection of I-84 and the Taconic State Parkway directly below.

2.5   Pass through large hemlock grove, and continue to descend.

2.9   Blue-blazed side trail to left leads 0.4 mile to Bailey Spring, a water source, with adjacent **campsites**.

3.2   Reach paved Hosner Mountain Road. Cross road, then cross bridge over small brook, and begin gradual ascent, passing through hemlock grove.

3.4 Make sharp right turn, then ascend steeply, climbing rock steps.

3.8 Reach viewpoint to left, over the Hudson River Valley, at the first summit of Stormville Mountain. Soon, begin descent.

4.0 At base of descent, pass old trail to left, then begin ascent of second summit of Stormville Mountain.

4.3 Reach second summit of Stormville Mountain, and begin descent on switchbacks.

4.8 Reach paved N.Y. 52 (end of section). To continue, turn left (north) on N.Y. 52 for 125 feet, then cross road, and reenter woods (see New York Section Four).

Taconic State Parkway to N.Y. 301
New York Section Six
7.2 Miles

Brief Description of Section

The Trail in this section passes over the summit of Shenandoah Mountain, with many good views on both sides of the Trail. The southern portion of the section passes through Clarence Fahnestock Memorial State Park, with a beautiful viewpoint over Canopus Lake. The elevation at the Taconic State Parkway is 540 feet; at N.Y. 301, it is 930 feet. The highest elevation on the section is 1,282 feet, at the summit of Shenandoah Mountain.

Road Approaches

Both the northern and southern ends of this section are accessible by vehicle. At the northern end, the Trail crosses the Taconic State Parkway at Miller Hill Road. No parking is available at the parkway crossing, but limited parking is available at the Trail crossing of Hortontown Road, 0.4 mile from the northern end of the section. At the southern end of the section, the Trail crosses N.Y. 301 at the southern tip of Canopus Lake in Fahnestock State Park, 1.5 miles southwest of the junction of N.Y. 301 and the Taconic State Parkway. Ample parking is available 0.2 mile northeast of the Trail crossing on N.Y. 301. The Trail is also accessible from Long Hill Road, which crosses the Trail 2.7 miles from the northern end of the section.

Public Transportation

Public transportation is unavailable at either end of this section.

Maps

For route navigation, refer to Map Two with this guide. For area detail, refer to the following USGS 7½-minute topographic quadrangles: Hopewell Junction and Oscawana Lake, New York. Another good reference is NY-NJ TC East Hudson Trails Map No. 3.

Shelters and Campsites

This section of the Trail has one shelter:

RPH Shelter: Established by Ralph's Peak Hikers, formerly a local hiking club; located at the Trail crossing of Hortontown Road, 0.3 mile from northern end of section; 6.9 miles from southern end of section; accommodates 15 in three-sided cinder-block buildings with bunks; caretaker on duty in evenings from May to September; water and privy available. This shelter may be used by thru-hikers as a mail drop; packages will be held by the caretaker if sent to the shelter address (275A Hortontown Road, Hopewell Junction, NY 12533).

Next shelter: north 9.0 miles (Morgan Stewart Memorial Shelter); south 30.8 miles (West Mountain Shelter).

In addition, a campground is located near the southern end of the section:

Fahnestock State Park Campsites: Maintained by Fahnestock State Park; on the southern side of N.Y. 301, 1.0 mile northeast of the Trail crossing at the southern end of the section; hot showers, flush toilets, and rain shelters available; no fee for thru-hikers.

Supplies and Services

At the northern end of the section, groceries are available in Shenandoah, on Miller Hill Road, 1.2 miles north of the intersection of Miller Hill Road with the Taconic State Parkway.

In addition, a seasonal hot-dog and ice-cream stand is located at the beach at the northern end of Canopus Lake. Cold showers and swimming are also available. From the viewpoint overlooking Canopus Lake (4.9 miles from the northern end of the section, 2.3 miles from the southern end), follow unmarked trail steeply down to lake shore, then proceed for about 0.2 mile along shore.

Public Accommodations

No accommodations are available in this section.

Trail Description, North to South

Miles	Data

Miles   **Data**

0.0 From Taconic State Parkway at Miller Hill Road, proceed west on Miller Hill Road for 250 feet, then turn left, and enter woods.

0.1 Cross bridge over brook. Descend through hemlock grove between stone walls.

0.2 Turn right, and cross stone wall.

0.3 Descend rock steps, and cross Hortontown Road. In another 200 feet, side trail to left leads to **RPH Shelter.**

0.4 Cross bridge over brook, then follow puncheon over swampy area. Begin to ascend, crossing several stone walls.

0.6 Cross stream, and begin steep ascent.

0.8 Trail levels off.

1.0 Pass through hemlock grove.

1.2 Cross stream, and continue ascent.

1.3 Reach summit, with views through trees to east, then begin descent.

1.6 Begin steep ascent.

1.7 Turn right at viewpoint to east, and soon resume ascending rather steeply.

1.9 Pass through gap in stone wall.

2.0 Trail levels off and soon begins to descend.

2.1 Cross clearing for powerlines.

2.4 Cross intermittent stream.

2.5 Begin to ascend.

2.7 Cross Long Hill Road, and continue steady ascent.

3.0 To right of Trail is viewpoint to west.

3.1 Reach open summit of Shenandoah Mountain (1,282 feet), with beautiful views to east and views through trees to west. Begin descent.

3.5 Trail levels off and joins old woods road, with stone wall to left.

4.1 Cross intermittent stream, and continue along stone wall, soon passing ruins of old building.

4.2 Turn right, and leave road.

4.4   Cross small stream.
4.6   Begin to ascend rather steeply, then more moderately.
4.7   Trail levels off.
4.8   Side trail leads to viewpoint to west through trees. In another 275 feet, reach improved viewpoint to west.
4.9   Reach beautiful viewpoint over Canopus Lake, at north end of lake. Begin descent, steeply in places.
5.2   Cross small stream. Continue to parallel west shore of lake, with views of the lake below, through the trees.
6.3   Cross rocky stream, and continue along ridge shoulder on western side of Canopus Lake.
6.8   Begin descent to N.Y. 301.
6.9   Please sign Trail register located on tree to left of Trail. In another 100 feet, the Trail descends steeply.
7.1   Reach N.Y. 301. Turn left, and follow road.
7.2   Reach southern end of Canopus Lake (end of section). To continue, cross road, and reenter woods (see New York Section Seven).

Trail Description, South to North

Miles   **Data**

0.0   From southern end of Canopus Lake, proceed west along N.Y. 301.
0.1   Turn right, and enter woods, descending gently.
0.3   After steep ascent, turn right and, in another 100 feet, please sign Trail register located on tree to right of Trail.
0.4   Trail levels off, then begins to descend.
0.9   Cross rocky stream, and continue to parallel west shore of lake, with some views of the lake through the trees.
2.0   Cross small stream.
2.2   Begin steep climb.
2.3   Reach beautiful viewpoint over Canopus Lake at northern end of lake.
2.4   Reach viewpoint to west. In another 275 feet, side trail leads to another viewpoint to west.
2.5   Begin descent, first moderately, and then more steeply.

2.8   Cross small stream.
3.0   Turn left, and join old woods road bordered by stone walls.
3.1   Pass ruins of old building. Cross intermittent stream, and continue along stone wall.
3.7   Leave woods road, and begin to ascend.
4.1   Reach open summit of Shenandoah Mountain (1,282 feet), with beautiful views to east and views through trees to west. Begin to descend.
4.2   Viewpoint to west is to left of Trail. Continue steady descent.
4.5   Cross Long Hill Road, and continue to descend.
4.7   Trail levels off.
4.8   Cross intermittent stream.
5.1   Cross clearing for powerlines.
5.2   Begin descent.
5.3   Pass through gap in stone wall, and continue to descend, steeply in places.
5.5   Turn left at viewpoint to east, and descend steeply.
5.9   After ascent, reach summit, with views through trees to east, then begin descent.
6.0   Cross stream, and continue descent.
6.2   Pass through hemlock grove.
6.4   Begin steep descent.
6.6   Cross stream, then continue a more gradual descent, crossing several stone walls.
6.8   Follow puncheon over swampy area, and cross bridge over brook. In another 400 feet, side trail to right leads to **RPH Shelter.**
6.9   Cross Hortontown Road, and ascend rock steps.
7.0   Cross stone wall. Turn left, follow path between two stone walls, and ascend. Soon, pass through hemlocks.
7.1   Cross bridge over brook. In another 250 feet, turn right onto Miller Hill Road.
7.2   Reach Taconic State Parkway (end of section). To continue, cross parkway, and turn left onto unpaved Rock Ledge Road (see New York Section Five).

N.Y. 301 to Canopus Hill Road
New York Section Seven
7.4 Miles

Brief Description of Section

Most of this section is in the Clarence Fahnestock Memorial State Park, donated to the state of New York in 1929 by Dr. Ernest Fahnestock in memory of his brother. At the northern end, the Trail follows a narrow-gauge railroad bed built in 1862 to transport ore from Sunk Mine to Cold Spring Turnpike. Elevation at N.Y. 301 is 930 feet; at Canopus Hill Road, 420 feet. The highest point is 1,061 feet, on the ridge between Sunk Mine Road and Dennytown Road.

Road Approaches

Both the northern and southern ends of this section are accessible by vehicle. At the northern end, the Trail crosses N.Y. 301 at the southern tip of Canopus Lake in Fahnestock State Park, 1.5 miles southwest of the junction of N.Y. 301 and the Taconic State Parkway. Parking is available on N.Y. 301, 0.2 mile northeast of the Trail crossing.

The southern end is on Canopus Hill Road, 0.3 mile west of its intersection with Canopus Hollow Road at Canopus Valley Crossroads. Take U.S. 9 to Travis Corners Road. Proceed east on Travis Corners Road 0.8 mile to Old Albany Post Road. Turn right onto Old Albany Post Road, then left at the next intersection onto Canopus Hill Road. Continue east on Canopus Hill Road for one mile to the Trail crossing. Parking is not available here but is available at Dennytown Road, which intersects the A.T. 3.6 miles from the northern end of the section and 3.8 miles from the southern end. To reach this point, follow Dennytown Road south from N.Y. 301 for about 1.2 miles.

Public Transportation

Public transportation is unavailable at either end of this section.

Maps

For route navigation, refer to Map Two with this guide. For area detail, refer to the following USGS 7½-minute topographic quadrangle: Oscawana Lake, New York. Another reference is NY-NJ TC East Hudson Trails Map No. 3.

Shelters and Campsites

This section of the Trail has two camping areas:

Fahnestock State Park Campsites: Maintained by Fahnestock State Park; on the southern side of N.Y. 301, 1.0 mile northeast of the Trail crossing at the northern end of the section. Hot showers, flush toilets, and rain shelters available; no fee for thru-hikers.

Dennytown Road Group Campsites: Maintained by Fahnestock State Park, on Dennytown Road at the Trail crossing, 3.6 miles from the northern end of the section, and 3.8 miles from the southern end of the section. Water and latrines are available; only for thru-hikers; no fee.

Supplies and Services

Supplies and services are unavailable in this section.

Public Accommodations

No accommodations are available in this section.

Trail Description, North to South

Miles   **Data**

0.0   From N.Y. 301, enter hemlock grove, and follow bed of old mine railway, with Canopus Creek to left.

0.7   Trail turns left and leaves railway bed, as yellow-blazed Old Mine Railroad Trail continues straight ahead along railway bed.

0.9   Cross blue-blazed Three Lakes Trail. (To left, Three Lakes Trail leads back to N.Y. 301.)

1.1   Bear left, descend into small hollow, and ascend over knoll.

1.3   Enter level area that was once a farm. Turn right, away from swamp. In 50 yards, turn left, and ascend through hemlocks.

1.6   Reach top of ridge. Continue along ridge through hemlocks, with some good views on both sides.

1.9   Descend short, steep cliff. Ascend slightly, then level off.

2.0   Cross bridge over stream, outlet of swamp to right of Trail.

2.1   Reach Sunk Mine Road. Turn right along road briefly, then turn left into woods, and begin to ascend. Sunk Mine Road continues to a junction with the Three Lakes Trail, which can be used as an alternate route back to N.Y. 301.

2.7   Reach height of land, with western view. Trail begins to descend, with views to south and east.

3.4   Cross swamp outlet, formerly a beaver pond, on right. Turn right, and continue above the southern edge of the pond.

3.6   Emerge onto large open field. Continue along left side of field, and reach Dennytown Road. **Dennytown Road Group Campsites** and water (from pump) are here. Cross road, and continue for 100 feet on joint route with blue-blazed Three Lakes Trail, then turn left as Three Lakes Trail continues straight ahead.

4.1   Reach limited viewpoint to east.

4.8   Cross red-blazed Catfish Loop Trail.

5.6   After steady descent, turn right onto woods road.

5.8   Turn sharp left, leaving woods road, and cross large boulder field. Begin to ascend, leaving Fahnestock State Park.

6.4   Cross bridge over stream, and turn right. In 150 feet, cross South Highland Road (Philipse Brook Road), and ascend stone steps on opposite side of road.

7.4   Reach dirt Canopus Hill Road (end of section). To continue, cross road, and follow Trail into woods (see New York Section Eight).

Trail Description, South to North

Miles	Data

0.0   From Canopus Hill Road, proceed north on Trail.

1.0   Reach South Highland Road (Philipse Brook Road). Cross road, and bear right, paralleling road for 150 feet, then turn left, and cross bridge over stream.

1.3   Reach height of land, and begin to descend.

1.5   Enter Fahnestock State Park, and cross large boulder field.

1.6   Turn right onto woods road.

1.8   Just before reaching stream with broken-down bridge, turn sharp left, leaving woods road. Reenter woods, and begin steady descent.

2.5   Cross red-blazed Catfish Loop Trail.

3.2   Reach limited viewpoint to east.

3.8   After briefly following joint route with blue-blazed Three Lakes Trail, which comes in from left, reach Dennytown Road. **Dennytown Road Group Campsites** and water (from pump) are here. Cross road, and follow along right edge of large open field, then turn sharp right, and reenter woods.

4.0   After passing swamp, formerly a beaver pond, to left of Trail, turn left, as red-blazed Catfish Loop Trail leaves to right. Follow east edge of swamp, then cross its outlet stream.

4.2   Ascend ridge, with views to south and east.

4.7   Reach high point of ridge, with view to west, and begin descent.

5.3   Reach Sunk Mine Road. Turn right along road briefly, then turn left into woods. To the left, Sunk Mine Road leads to blue-blazed Three Lakes Trail.

5.4   Cross bridge over stream, outlet of swamp to left of Trail.

5.5   Ascend face of short, steep cliff, then continue along ridge, through hemlocks, with some good views on both sides.

6.0   At base of descent, enter level area that was once a farm. Turn right toward swamp, then, in 50 yards, turn left, and ascend over knoll.

6.3   Ascend steeply, and bear right.

6.5   Cross blue-blazed Three Lakes Trail (to right, Three Lakes Trail provides an alternate route to N.Y. 301).

6.7   A.T. turns right and follows old mine-railway bed. Yellow-blazed Old Mine Railroad Trail begins here and follows bed of old mine railway to left. Canopus Creek soon becomes visible to the right.

7.4   Pass through hemlock grove, and reach N.Y. 301 (end of section). To continue, turn left along N.Y. 301 (see New York Section Six).

Canopus Hill Road to U.S. 9
New York Section Eight
5.0 Miles

Brief Description of Section

The Trail in this section climbs over Canopus Hill and continues over Denning Hill and Little Fort Hill—a ridge of hills full of history. It crosses the Old Albany Post Road, which was the main land route from New York to Albany during the Revolutionary War.

This area saw considerable activity during the Revolutionary War. The Canopus Valley and Old Albany post roads were used by the Continentals to travel from Fishkill, a military supply depot, to Continental Village. The latter was the site of a troop encampment and still remains a small village. On October 9, 1777, the British moved north from Peekskill and routed the 2,000 Continentals camped there. The men took to the surrounding hills, most of which were fortified. The names on the land—Fort Hill, Little Fort Hill, Fort Defiance Hill, Gallows Hill—are reminders of that time. The Old West Point Road led to Benedict Arnold's headquarters at Garrison. It was also one of the roads taken by the military escort of Major André, then a captive, from headquarters in North Salem to Garrison, after the flight of the traitorous Arnold.

The elevation at Canopus Hill Road is 420 feet; at U.S. 9, it is 400 feet. The highest elevation is 900 feet, at the top of Denning Hill.

Road Approaches

Both the northern and southern ends of this section are accessible by vehicle. Parking is not available at the northern end, where the Trail crosses Canopus Hill Road 0.3 mile west of its intersection with Canopus Hollow Road at Canopus Valley Crossroads. At the southern end, the Trail crosses U.S. 9 at its intersection with N.Y. 403, 0.5 mile north of the Graymoor Monastery and 4.0 miles north of the U.S. 9-U.S. 6/202 intersection just north of Peekskill. Parking is available on a short road between U.S. 9 and N.Y. 403, about 0.1 mile north of the Trail crossing.

Public Transportation

Public transportation is unavailable at either end of the section.

Maps

For route navigation, refer to Map Two with this guide. For area detail, refer to the following USGS 7½-minute topographic quadrangles: West Point and Peekskill, New York. Additional references are NY-NJ TC East Hudson Trails Maps No. 1 and 3.

Shelters and Campsites

No shelters or campsites are available in this section.

Supplies and Services

At the southern end of the section, meals may be obtained at the Bavarian Inn on U.S. 9, 0.8 mile south of the Trail crossing. Groceries and sandwiches are available at a store located at the intersection of U.S. 9 and South Mountain Pass, 1.9 miles south of the Trail crossing (open seven days a week). A variety of supplies and services is available in Peekskill, about 4.8 miles from the southern end of the section. From the Trail crossing of U.S. 9, proceed south on U.S. 9 for 3.1 miles, then follow Highland Avenue to the center of Peekskill.

Public Accommodations

Motels are available in Peekskill, 4.8 miles from the southern end of the section.

Trail Description, North to South

Miles   **Data**

0.0   From Canopus Hill Road, follow Trail to south, entering woods on footpath.

0.1   Cross brook, turn right, and begin moderate ascent of Canopus Hill.

0.4   Bear right, pass large hemlock to left of Trail, and continue to ascend more steeply.

0.7   Reach viewpoint in cleared area at top of Canopus Hill. Trail turns right and levels off. In another 300 feet, begin steep descent through mountain laurel.

0.9   Cross several stone walls as Trail ascends slightly.

1.4   Pass through gap in stone wall.

1.6   Pass through blueberry patch, and begin rather steep descent.

1.7   After crossing wet area on rocks, reach dirt Chapman Road at its intersection with Old Albany Post Road. Cross road, and reenter woods. In 125 feet, cross swampy area on puncheon, and ascend.

1.8   Bear left, and continue along side of hill.

2.1   Descend steeply over rocks.

2.3   Ascend steeply along rocky area, then continue to ascend more gradually.

2.5   Cross stone wall, turn right, and ascend to viewpoint in clearing near top of Denning Hill, with good view to east. On a clear day, you can see New York City skyline. Continue along ridge for 150 feet, then turn left, and descend steeply.

2.8   Turn left onto woods road. Blue-blazed side trail to right leads 650 feet to an excellent view of the Hudson River.

2.9   Turn left, leaving woods road. Reenter woods on footpath, and pass through area burned in 1991 fire.

3.0   Short, unmarked trail to right leads to viewpoint. A.T. descends steeply over rocks and follows ridge of Little Fort Hill.

3.7   Short side trail marked with orange tin-can blazes leads left to shrine of Graymoor Monastery, with views to east.

4.3 After passing through overgrown field, reenter woods briefly, then emerge onto private gravel road. Turn right, and follow road uphill.

4.4 Cross paved Old West Point Road (paving ends at this point), and continue straight ahead along paved road. Follow road for 400 feet, passing farm building to right, then turn right, pass through grassy area, and enter woods, descending steeply for short distance.

4.5 Cross cleared strip of land, which curves to right, then continue along cleared strip.

4.6 Turn right, and reenter woods.

4.8 Cross dirt Old Highland Turnpike, then cross swampy area on puncheon.

5.0 Reach U.S. 9 (end of section). To continue, cross road, continue across cement island, cross N.Y. 403, cross stile over barbed-wire fence, and follow puncheon across pasture (see New York Section Nine).

Trail Description, South to North

Miles   **Data**

0.0 At intersection of U.S. 9 with N.Y. 403, proceed east, and enter woods on footpath.

0.2 Cross swampy area on puncheon, then cross dirt Old Highland Turnpike. Continue on footpath through woods.

0.4 Turn left, and follow cleared strip of land.

0.5 After brief, steep ascent, pass through grassy area, and turn left onto paved road.

0.6 Cross paved Old West Point Road (paving ends at this point), and continue downhill on private gravel road.

0.7 Turn left off gravel road, and reenter woods on footpath. Pass through overgrown field, and begin ascent of Little Fort Hill.

1.3 Short side trail marked with orange tin-can blazes leads right to shrine of Graymoor Monastery, with views to east.

1.8 Pass through area burned in 1991 fire.

2.0 At top of rocky ascent, short, unmarked trail to left leads to viewpoint.

2.1   Turn right onto woods road.

2.2   Turn right, and leave woods road. To the left, the woods road (blue-blazed) leads in 650 feet to an excellent view of the Hudson River.

2.5   After short, steep ascent, reach ridge of Denning Hill. Turn right, and continue along ridge for 150 feet to viewpoint in clearing, with good view to east. On a clear day, you can see New York City skyline. From clearing, continue briefly along stone wall, then turn left, and descend.

2.7   Descend steeply along rocky area.

2.9   Ascend steeply over rocks, then continue along side of hill.

3.3   After descending, cross swampy area on puncheon, and, in 125 feet, reach dirt Old Albany Post Road at its intersection with Chapman Road. Cross road diagonally to left, and reenter woods. Cross wet area on rocks, then ascend rather steeply.

3.4   Pass through blueberry patch as Trail levels off.

3.6   Pass through gap in stone wall.

4.0   Cross several stone walls.

4.2   Turn right, and ascend steeply through mountain laurel.

4.3   Reach top of Canopus Hill. Trail levels off. In another 300 feet, reach viewpoint in cleared area. Trail turns left and begins steep descent.

4.6   Pass large hemlock tree to right of Trail. Continue to descend, but more moderately.

4.9   Cross brook.

5.0   Reach dirt Canopus Hill Road (end of section). To continue, cross road, and follow Trail north into woods (see New York Section Seven).

U.S. 9 to Bear Mountain Bridge
New York Section Nine
5.8 Miles

Brief Description of Section

This section of the Trail passes through varied terrain. The northern end is a walk on trails and old carriage roads through woodland, with a magnificent viewpoint over the Hudson River. The southern part of the section includes a steep descent of the ridge of Anthony's Nose, with views across the river to the west. The Hudson Highlands can be seen at the crossing of the Bear Mountain Bridge. At the time of its completion in 1924, the Bear Mountain Bridge was the longest suspension bridge in the world. It has been designated a national engineering landmark. The elevation at U.S. 9 is 400 feet and, at the Bear Mountain Bridge, 176 feet. The highest elevation is 840 feet on Canada Hill.

On Canada Hill, the Trail winds through Hudson Highlands State Park. Numerous old carriage roads are found in the park; some are even used for the Trail. Do not be surprised to see evidence of horses in this area, as they are permitted on the carriage roads (but not on the trails).

Many legends speculate on the naming of Anthony's Nose. Some early historians believed it was named in 1525 by Estevan Gomez, a Portuguese sailor, who referred to the river as "Rio St. Antonio." In fact, the village of Manitou, north of the bridge, was once called St. Anthonysville. Washington Irving's version in Diedrich Knickerbocker's *History of New York* claims it was named for Anthony Van Corlear, or Anthony the Trumpeter. Some believe that it was named for General "Mad" Anthony Wayne, who, among other exploits, led the successful march to capture the fort at Stony Point from the British in 1779. (A Bicentennial Trail in the Bear Mountain-Harriman State Parks follows the march's route.) Two forts, Clinton and Montgomery, were built on either side of where the Bear Mountain Bridge now stands.

Road Approaches

At the northern end of the section, the Trail crosses U.S. 9 at its intersection with N.Y. 403, 0.5 mile north of the Graymoor Monastery and 4.0 miles north of the intersection of U.S. 9 with U.S. 6/202, just north of Peekskill. Parking is available on a short road between U.S. 9 and N.Y. 403, about 0.1 mile north of the Trail crossing.

The southern end of the section is at the tollgate at the western end of the Bear Mountain Bridge. No parking is available here, but parking is available along the shoulder of N.Y. 9D about 0.2 mile south of the point where the Trail leaves N.Y. 9D and ascends Anthony's Nose. Parking is also available at the Bear Mountain Inn, 0.8 mile south of the tollgate (fee charged in summer).

Note that this area has three Route 9s. U.S. 9, which crosses the Trail at the northern end of the section, is also known as the New York-Albany Post Road. N.Y. 9D, which is followed by the Trail at the southern end of the section, runs parallel to and near the Hudson River on the eastern side of the river and ends at the Bear Mountain Bridge. U.S. 9W is on the western side of the river.

Public Transportation

At the southern end of the section, bus service to New York City via Short Line Bus System, (201) 529-3666, is available at the Bear Mountain Inn, 0.8 mile to the south on the Trail. Limited rail service (weekends only) to New York City (Grand Central Terminal) via the Metro-North Commuter Railroad, (212) 532-4900 or (800) 638-7646, is available at Manitou, 1.6 miles north of the point where the Trail leaves N.Y. 9D and ascends Anthony's Nose. (Walk north on N.Y. 9D for 1.0 mile, then turn left on Manitou Road, and follow it for 0.6 mile to the station.)

No public transportation is available at the northern end of the section.

Maps

For route navigation, refer to Maps Two and Three with this guide. For area detail, refer to the following USGS 7½-minute topographic quadrangle: Peekskill, New York. Another reference is NY-NJ TC East Hudson Trails Map No. 1.

Shelters and Campsites

This section has one campsite:

Hemlock Springs Campsite: 3.6 miles from northern end of section; 2.2 miles from southern end of section; water available from spring.

Supplies and Services

At the northern end of the section, meals may be obtained at the Bavarian Inn on U.S. 9, 0.8 mile south of the Trail crossing. Groceries and sandwiches are available at a store located at the intersection of U.S. 9 and South Mountain Pass, 1.9 miles south of the Trail crossing (open seven days a week). This store may also be reached from the Trail crossing of South Mountain Pass, 2.4 miles from the southern end of the section, by following South Mountain Pass east for 1.7 miles to U.S. 9.

At the southern end, meals are available at the Bear Mountain Inn, 0.8 mile south of the tollgate of the Bear Mountain Bridge. A post office (ZIP Code 10911) is near the inn. Fort Montgomery has meals, groceries, and a post office (ZIP Code 10922) 0.7 mile north of the Bear Mountain Bridge tollgate on U.S. 9W.

A variety of supplies and services is available in Peekskill, about four to five miles south of the Trail. From the Trail crossing of U.S. 9, walk south on U.S. 9 for 3.1 miles, then follow Highland Avenue to the center of Peekskill. From the eastern end of Bear Mountain Bridge, follow U.S. 6/202 to the center of town.

Public Accommodations

At the southern end of the section, accommodations are available at the Bear Mountain Inn, 0.8 mile to the south, and in Fort Montgomery, 0.7 mile to the north. Motels are available in Peekskill, 4.0 miles south of the southern end of the section and 4.8 miles south of the northern end.

Trail Description, North to South

Miles   **Data**

0.0   At intersection of U.S. 9 with N.Y. 403, cross stile over
        barbed-wire fence on the west side of N.Y. 403, and follow
        puncheon across pasture. Cross second stile over barbed-
        wire fence, then bear left, and follow old woods road, with
        stone wall to left.

0.1   Turn right onto old carriage road.

0.5   At wood steps on left side of the road, turn left, and
        ascend, steeply in places, on footpath into woods.

1.0   Turn left onto old carriage road, and continue along ridge
        of Canada Hill. (To the right is one end of the blue-blazed
        Osborn Loop Trail, which rejoins the A.T. at the southern
        end of the Canada Hill Ridge at mile 2.4. The Osborn Loop
        Trail passes Sugarloaf, which has good views of the Hud-
        son River.)

1.1   Blue-blazed side trail to right leads 100 feet to beautiful
        viewpoint over Hudson River, with Bear Mountain Bridge
        visible to left and West Point visible to the right.

1.9   Unmarked side trail to right leads to Manitoga Nature
        Preserve.

2.3   Trail curves to the right as unmarked trail goes off to left.

2.4   Please sign the Trail register on tree to right of Trail. Turn
        left, and leave old carriage road, continuing on footpath.
        (Straight ahead, old carriage road is the other end of the
        Osborn Loop Trail, which leads to Manitoga Nature Pre-
        serve.)

3.0   Begin steady descent.

3.4   Reach South Mountain Pass (a dirt road). Turn right, and
        follow road downhill for 250 feet, then turn left onto dirt
        road obstructed by large rocks.

3.6   Turn right off dirt road. In 100 feet, blue-blazed trail to left
        leads to **Hemlock Springs Campsite** and spring (a water
        source). A.T. descends steeply on footpath.

3.7   Cross brook, pass through hemlock grove, and begin to
        ascend, first steeply, then moderately.

3.9   With stone embankment of road in sight ahead, curve to the right, and continue to ascend on switchbacks.

4.1   Reach viewpoint to west and north over Hudson River. Continue straight ahead, descending gradually. Avoid unmarked side trail to right.

4.4   Reach rocky dirt road. Continue straight ahead on dirt road.

4.6   Turn right off dirt road, and descend steeply on footpath. Dirt road leads ahead to summit of Anthony's Nose, with magnificent views of Bear Mountain, Bear Mountain Bridge, and Iona Island to west.

5.0   With N.Y. 9D visible directly below, turn left, and follow relatively level path to south, parallel to road.

5.1   Reach paved N.Y. 9D at Westchester-Putnam county line. Turn left, and follow road.

5.3   Turn right, and cross Bear Mountain Bridge. Excellent views north and south along Hudson River.

5.8   Reach tollgate at western end of bridge (end of section). To continue, turn left, and follow Trail through Trailside Museum and Zoo (see New York Section Ten).

Trail Description, South to North

Miles   **Data**

0.0   From tollgate on west side of Bear Mountain Bridge, proceed across bridge. Excellent views north and south along Hudson River.

0.5   At east end of bridge, turn left (north) on N.Y. 9D.

0.7   At Westchester-Putnam county line, turn right, leaving N.Y. 9D, and enter woods on footpath. Trail climbs, often steeply, up Anthony's Nose.

1.2   Reach dirt road. Turn left, and follow road. To right, road leads to summit of Anthony's Nose, with magnificent views of Bear Mountain, Bear Mountain Bridge, and Iona Island to west.

1.4   As dirt road curves to right, continue straight ahead on footpath. Trail ascends gradually.

1.7   Reach viewpoint to west and north over Hudson River. Continue straight ahead, and begin to descend. Avoid unmarked side trail to left.

1.9   With stone embankment of road in sight ahead, Trail curves to left and continues to descend, first moderately and then more steeply.

2.1   Make sharp right turn, soon continue descent, and pass through hemlock grove. Cross brook, and begin steep ascent.

2.2   Blue-blazed trail to right leads to **Hemlock Springs Campsite** and to spring (water source). In another 100 feet, turn left on dirt road, and begin steady descent.

2.4   Reach South Mountain Pass (a dirt road). Turn right, and follow road uphill for 250 feet, then turn left, reenter woods on footpath, and begin steady ascent of Canada Hill.

2.8   Trail levels off.

3.4   Reach junction with old carriage road, with Trail register on tree. Please sign Trail register. Turn right. (To left, carriage road is the blue-blazed Osborn Loop Trail, which leads to Manitoga Nature Preserve and rejoins the A.T. at the northern end of Canada Hill ridge, at mile 4.8.)

3.5   Trail curves to left. Continue ahead as unmarked trail goes off to right.

3.9   Unmarked side trail to left leads to Manitoga Nature Preserve.

4.7   Blue-blazed side trail to left leads in 100 feet to beautiful viewpoint over Hudson River, with Bear Mountain Bridge visible to the left and West Point visible to the right.

4.8   Turn right into woods, leaving old carriage road, and descend, steeply in places. (Straight ahead, old carriage road is the other end of the Osborn Loop Trail. It leads to Sugarloaf, which has good views of the Hudson River.)

5.3   Turn right onto old carriage road, and continue gradual descent.

5.7   At corner of fenced-in pasture, turn left onto old woods road.

5.8 Cross stile over barbed-wire fence. Follow puncheon across pasture, then cross second stile over barbed-wire fence, and reach N.Y. 403. Continue across cement island, and reach U.S. 9 (end of section). To continue, cross road, and reenter woods on the other side of the guardrail (see New York Section Eight).

Bear Mountain Bridge to
Arden Valley Road (Tiorati Circle)
New York Section Ten
13.3 Miles

Brief Description of Section

This section passes through the northern portion of Harriman-Bear Mountain State Parks. From the Bear Mountain Bridge at the northern end of the section, the Trail descends to an elevation of 124 feet in the Trailside Museum—the lowest elevation on the entire A.T. It then climbs to the summit of Bear Mountain (1,305 feet), marked by the Perkins Tower, and later crosses West, Black, Letterrock, and Goshen mountains. Many beautiful views can be seen from the summits and ridges of these mountains.

The portion of the A.T. crossing Harriman State Park was the first section of the Trail to be completed. It officially opened on Sunday, October 7, 1923.

Financier and railroad magnate Edward R. Harriman (1848-1909) conceived the idea of establishing a park in this area. After his death, the park became a reality. In 1908, the State of New York acquired land around Bear Mountain to erect a prison. Due to the historical significance and scenic beauty of this land, the public objected to this proposal. Finally, in 1910, Harriman's widow, Mary A. Harriman, agreed to donate 10,000 acres of land to the state on the condition the state abandon its plan to establish a prison at Bear Mountain. Harriman-Bear Mountain Parks expanded considerably in succeeding years, and many improvements were made under the supervision of Major William Welch, general manager and chief engineer of the park from 1910 to 1940. Major Welch designed the diamond-shaped metal marker that became the standard symbol of the Appalachian Trail. He also served as the first chairman of the Appalachian Trail Conference.

The Trailside Museum, opened in 1927, fulfilled, in part, Benton MacKaye's dream of establishing nature trails and museums all along the A.T. This is the only such facility ever built along the Trail.

During very dry periods, trails in the park may be closed to the public to prevent forest fires; however, the A.T. may remain open. During such periods, hikers are advised to consult the staff members at the park's headquarters at Bear Mountain or at the stone building at the Tiorati Circle for current information on the status of the trails in the park.

For descriptions of the various trails crossing the A.T. in this section, as well as other trails in the immediate vicinity, consult *Harriman Trails: A Guide and History*, published by the New York-New Jersey Trail Conference.

Road Approaches

Both the northern and southern ends of this section are accessible by vehicle. The northern end is at the tollgate at the western end of the Bear Mountain Bridge. No parking is available here, but ample parking is available at the Bear Mountain Inn, 0.8 mile to the south (fee charged in summer). At the southern end, the Trail crosses Arden Valley Road 0.3 mile west of its intersection with Seven Lakes Drive at the Tiorati Circle. No parking is available at the Trail crossing, but ample parking is available at the Tiorati Circle (fee charged in summer).

Public Transportation

At the northern end of the section, bus service to New York City via Short Line Bus System, (201) 529-3666, is available at the Bear Mountain Inn, 0.8 mile to the south on the Trail. No public transportation is available at the southern end of the section.

Maps

For route navigation, refer to Map Three with this guide. For area detail, refer to the following USGS 7½-minute topographic quadrangles: Peekskill and Popolopen Lake, New York. Another reference is NY-NJ TC Trail Map No. 4 (Harriman Park-North Half).

Shelters and Campsites

This section has two shelters:

West Mountain Shelter: Stone structure; built in 1928; 5.8 miles from northern end of section; 7.5 miles from southern end of section; 0.6 mile from the A.T. on blue-blazed Timp-Torne Trail; accommodates 8; water may be available from unreliable spring 0.4 mile farther on Timp-Torne Trail (steep descent required—not recommended).

Next shelter: north 30.8 miles (RPH Shelter); south 3.3 miles.

William Brien Memorial Shelter: Stone structure; built in 1933 by Civilian Conservation Corps; 9.1 miles from northern end of section; 4.2 miles from southern end of section; accommodates 8; water from spring-fed well on blue-blazed trail (may fail in dry weather). This shelter is named in memory of the first president of the New York Ramblers, William Brien, who bequeathed funds to erect a shelter on the A.T. The original shelter at Island Pond was removed and the name transferred to this shelter on Letterrock Mountain.

Next shelter: north 3.3 miles; south 5.3 miles (Fingerboard Shelter).

Supplies and Services

At the northern end of the section, meals are available at the Bear Mountain Inn, 0.8 mile to the south along the Trail. A post office (ZIP Code 10911) and the headquarters of Harriman-Bear Mountain State Parks are near the inn. Meals, groceries, and a post office (ZIP Code 10922) are available in the village of Fort Montgomery, 0.7 mile to the north along U.S. 9W.

At the southern end, refreshments may be obtained during the summer at the Tiorati Circle, 0.3 mile east of the Trail crossing of Arden Valley Road. A ranger station, bathing beach, and a public phone are located at the Tiorati Circle. Water is available from early May until November 1 from a faucet at the northeast corner of the circle.

Public Accommodations

At the northern end of the section, accommodations are available at the Bear Mountain Inn and in Fort Montgomery, 0.7 mile to the north along U.S. 9W.

Trail Description, North to South

Miles   Data

0.0   From tollgate at west end of Bear Mountain Bridge, turn
        left, pass through gate in fence, and enter Trailside Mu-
        seum and Zoo. Reach nature and geology museums and
        Fort Clinton Historical Museum, then bear right, and
        follow paved path through zoo, past exhibits and memo-
        rials, including a statue of Walt Whitman. (If gate is closed
        after 5 p.m., continue straight ahead to traffic circle, bear
        left, cross U.S. 9W, and proceed to Hessian Lake straight
        ahead. Then turn left, and follow paved path along eastern
        shore of lake until A.T. is reached toward southern end of
        lake.)

0.3   Pass through gate, and leave Trailside Museum and Zoo.
        Immediately turn right, passing refreshment stand on
        right. Then, turn right for 250 feet, turn left, and cross
        under U.S. 9W via underpass. Walk up steps, turn left, and
        follow paved path for 125 feet. Then, turn left on another
        paved path.

0.6   Turn right toward lake. (Paved path straight ahead leads
        to Bear Mountain Inn.) After 100 feet, turn left, and con-
        tinue on another paved path along eastern shore of Hes-
        sian Lake.

0.8   Reach playground area at southern end of lake. Turn left,
        cutting diagonally across playground, and reach junction
        of paved paths. Here, Major Welch, Cornell, and Suffern-
        Bear Mountain (S-BM) trails begin. (Major Welch Trail
        provides an alternate route up Bear Mountain.) Bear right,
        and follow paved path (jointly with yellow-blazed S-BM
        Trail) uphill.

1.0   Cross under ski jump.

1.1   Bear right onto crushed-stone road. In another 150 feet, continue straight ahead as crushed-stone road curves to right.

1.2   Turn left, and cross stream.

1.4   Turn right, leaving S-BM Trail (which continues straight ahead).

1.8   Reach old paved road, the former route of Perkins Drive (now abandoned), and turn right. In 150 feet, reach dead-end turnaround of Scenic Drive, and continue straight ahead on road, with beautiful views to right of Hudson River, Bear Mountain Bridge, Bear Mountain Inn, and Iona Island.

2.1   Turn left, and climb rock steps. Continue to ascend, with more views of the Hudson River and Iona Island.

2.3   Cross Scenic Drive.

2.4   Cross Scenic Drive again.

2.6   Pass plaque commemorating Joseph Bartha, pioneer trail builder, and reach summit of Bear Mountain (1,305 feet) at base of Perkins Memorial Tower, built in 1934 in memory of George W. Perkins, first president of the Palisades Interstate Park Commission. Beautiful views south to New York City skyline, west to Ramapo Hills, and east over Hudson Highlands. Turn left, and continue along edge of paved road.

2.7   Turn left, leave paved road, and begin steady descent.

3.2   Reach paved Perkins Drive. Turn left, and follow road downhill.

3.7   Leave Perkins Drive, and turn right into woods.

4.2   Cross Seven Lakes Drive. Turn left on wide woods road, route of the 1777 Trail.

4.3   Turn right onto woods road, now a cross-country ski trail.

4.5   Fawn Trail, marked with bright red blazes, begins on right.

4.7   Turn right, leave woods road, and begin steep ascent of West Mountain.

5.0   Reach beautiful viewpoint to east and southeast over Bear Mountain and Hudson River.

5.1   Blue-blazed Timp-Torne (T-T) Trail comes in from right and runs concurrently with A.T. In another 200 feet, reach second viewpoint over Bear Mountain and Hudson River, then turn right, and cross to west side of ridge.

5.2 Reach first of a series of viewpoints to west from rocky ledges on the west side of West Mountain. Swimming pool of Anthony Wayne Recreation Area is visible directly below. Continue along west ridge of West Mountain.

5.4 Climb to top of long, flat rock, then turn right, and descend. In another 375 feet, turn left, and again come out on rocky ledges, with good views to west.

5.8 A.T. continues straight ahead as T-T Trail diverges to left. **West Mountain Shelter** is 0.6 mile ahead on T-T Trail. A.T. soon begins to descend.

6.3 Turn left onto grassy Beechy Bottom Road.

6.4 Turn right, leaving Beechy Bottom Road, and descend into woods. In another 75 feet, cross stream.

6.6 Red-on-white-blazed Ramapo-Dunderberg (R-D) Trail comes in from the left and runs concurrently with A.T. for next 3.3 miles. Please sign Trail register located on tree to the right of the Trail. A.T. continues along woods road, now a cross-country ski trail (with red blazes).

6.7 Turn right, leaving woods road, and continue on footpath. In another 200 feet, cross Beechy Bottom Brook, a water source.

7.0 Reach Palisades Interstate Parkway. Cross parkway, and reenter woods.

7.1 Cross old woods road.

7.3 Cross 1779 Trail, descend briefly, then begin ascent of Black Mountain, steeply in places.

7.7 Trail comes out on open rocks on south side of Black Mountain, with beautiful views of Hudson River to east. On a clear day, New York City is visible to the south. Continue across ridge of Black Mountain.

8.0 Begin to descend.

8.1 Reach viewpoint to northwest over Silvermine Lake. Descend steeply over rocky ridge.

8.2 Cross fire road, now a cross-country ski trail, and begin ascent of Letterrock Mountain.

9.1 Descend steeply over rocks, and reach **William Brien Memorial Shelter**. Blue-blazed trail to left leads 250 feet to spring-fed well, a water source (may fail in dry weather).

9.4   After ascent, reach rocky clearing, with views through trees to left.

9.9   At wooden bridge over wet area in saddle between Goshen and Letterrock mountains, A.T. turns right and proceeds over shoulder of Goshen Mountain as R-D Trail continues straight ahead to the Tiorati Circle.

10.1   Leave old woods road, and soon begin to descend gradually.

10.3   Make sharp right turn.

11.0   Turn left onto fire road.

11.1   Cross Seven Lakes Drive diagonally to the left, and reenter woods.

11.3   Cross bridge over stream, and begin ascent.

11.4   Cross cleared area, and continue to ascend.

11.5   Make sharp left turn, around switchback.

12.1   Reach rocky promontory; view to south over Lake Tiorati.

12.2   Turn left onto old woods road.

12.3   Turn left, and reenter woods. In another 300 feet, turn left, and rejoin woods road.

12.5   Leave woods road, and continue on footpath.

12.6   Cross woods road. Soon begin steady ascent.

12.9   Descend over rocks.

13.3   Reach Arden Valley Road (end of section). To continue, cross paved road, and reenter woods, following woods road (see New York Section Eleven).

Trail Description, South to North

Miles   Data

0.0   From crest of hill on Arden Valley Road, follow Trail north into woods.

0.4   Ascend over rocks. In another 250 feet, begin steady descent.

0.7   Cross woods road.

0.8   Join old woods road.

1.0   Turn right, and reenter woods. In another 300 feet, rejoin woods road coming in from left.

1.1   Turn right, leaving woods road.

1.2   Reach rocky promontory with view to south over Lake Tiorati; turn left into woods; soon begin steady descent.

1.8   Make sharp right turn, around switchback.

1.9   Cross cleared area. Trail soon levels off.

2.1   Cross bridge over stream.

2.2   Cross Seven Lakes Drive diagonally to the left, and follow grassy fire road into woods.

2.3   Turn right, leave fire road, and begin gradual ascent of shoulder of Goshen Mountain. (Fire road continues ahead to **William Brien Memorial Shelter**.)

3.0   Make sharp left turn.

3.2   Begin to descend on old woods road.

3.4   At the wooden bridge in the saddle between Goshen and Letterrock mountains, red-on-white-blazed Ramapo-Dunderberg (R-D) Trail comes in from right and joins A.T., running concurrently with it for the next 3.3 miles.

3.9   Reach rocky clearing, with views through trees to right, and begin to descend.

4.2   Cross old fire road, and reach **William Brien Memorial Shelter**. Blue-blazed trail to right leads 250 feet to spring-fed well, a water source (may fail in dry weather). Immediately after passing shelter, Trail climbs steeply up rocky ridge.

5.1   Cross fire road, now used as a cross-country ski trail, and ascend steeply over rocky ridge.

5.2   Reach viewpoint to northwest over Silvermine Lake.

5.3   Reach crest of Black Mountain, with views to south. Continue along crest of ridge.

5.5   Trail comes out on open rocks on south side of Black Mountain, with beautiful views of Hudson River to east. On a clear day, New York City may be visible to the south. Continue across ridge of Black Mountain, then begin steep descent.

6.0   Cross 1779 Trail.

6.2   Cross old woods road.

6.3   Reach Palisades Interstate Parkway. Cross parkway, and reenter woods.

6.5   Cross Beechy Bottom Brook, a water source.

6.6   Turn left, and join woods road, now a cross-country ski trail (with red blazes), which comes in from right.

6.7   Please sign Trail register located on tree to the left of the Trail. R-D Trail turns right at this point and leaves A.T. route.

6.8   Begin to ascend as Trail narrows to a footpath.

6.9   Cross stream. In another 75 feet, turn left onto grassy Beechy Bottom Road.

7.0   Turn right, leave Beechy Bottom Road, and ascend steeply up West Mountain.

7.5   Reach open rock ledges on west ridge of West Mountain. Blue-blazed Timp-Torne (T-T) Trail comes in from right and runs concurrently with A.T. **West Mountain Shelter** is 0.6 mile to right on T-T Trail. A.T. continues along west ridge of West Mountain, with many beautiful views to west.

7.9   Turn right, and soon climb to top of long, flat rock, then descend.

8.1   Again come out on open ledges on west ridge of West Mountain, with swimming pool of Anthony Wayne Recreation Area visible directly below. After reaching second open ledge, turn right, and cross to east side of ridge.

8.2   Reach beautiful viewpoint to east and southeast over Bear Mountain and Hudson River, then begin to descend. In another 200 feet, A.T. bears right at fork as T-T Trail continues straight ahead.

8.3   Reach second viewpoint over Bear Mountain and Hudson River. Continue to descend rather steeply.

8.6   Join old woods road, now a cross-country ski trail, which comes in from right, and continue gradual descent.

8.8   Fawn Trail, marked with bright red blazes, begins on left.

9.0   Turn left on wide woods road, route of 1777 Trail.

9.1   Turn right, and cross Seven Lakes Drive. Reenter woods, and begin ascent of Bear Mountain.

9.6   Reach paved Perkins Drive. Turn left, and follow paved road uphill.

10.1   Turn right off Perkins Drive, and reenter woods, ascending steadily.

10.6   Reach summit of Bear Mountain (1,305 feet) at base of Perkins Memorial Tower, built in 1934 in memory of George W. Perkins, first president of the Palisades Interstate Park Commission. Beautiful views south to New

York City skyline, west to Ramapo Hills, and east over Hudson Highlands. Turn right, and continue along edge of paved road.

10.7   Turn right, passing plaque commemorating Joseph Bartha, pioneer trail builder, and begin steady descent. In 150 feet, bear left on relocated Trail.

10.9   Cross paved Scenic Drive.

11.0   Cross Scenic Drive again, and continue to descend, with views ahead of Hudson River and Iona Island.

11.2   Turn right onto Scenic Drive. Continue along road, with beautiful views to the left of Hudson River, Bear Mountain Bridge, Bear Mountain Inn, and Iona Island.

11.5   Reach dead-end turnaround of Scenic Drive, and continue straight ahead on abandoned road, the former route of Perkins Drive. In another 150 feet, turn left, and descend steadily on footpath.

11.9   Turn left onto route of yellow-blazed Suffern-Bear Mountain (S-BM) Trail, which comes in from right and runs concurrently with A.T.

12.1   Cross stream, and turn right.

12.2   Join crushed-stone road coming in from left. In another 150 feet, join paved road coming in from right.

12.3   Cross under ski jump.

12.5   Reach intersection of paved paths at southern end of Hessian Lake. The S-BM Trail ends here, as do the Major Welch Trail (which provides an alternate route to the top of Bear Mountain) and the Cornell Trail. Paved path straight ahead leads to Bear Mountain Inn. Turn left, and cut diagonally across playground area, then turn right, and follow paved path along shore of Hessian Lake.

12.7   Turn right, away from shore, on paved path for 100 feet, then turn left, and follow another paved path parallel to Hessian Lake. (After five p.m., continue along shore path to end of Hessian Lake, then turn right, cross U.S. 9W, follow it around traffic circle, turn right, and continue to tollgate of Bear Mountain Bridge.)

12.8   Turn right, then walk down steps, and cross under U.S. 9W via underpass. Turn right on opposite side of underpass for 250 feet, then turn left, passing refreshment stand to left.

13.0   Turn left, and enter Trailside Museum and Zoo. (If gate is closed, follow U.S. 9W to north, and turn right at traffic circle to reach tollgate of Bear Mountain Bridge.) Pass exhibits and memorials, including a statue of Walt Whitman, and proceed through zoo.

13.3   Pass nature and geology museums and Fort Clinton Historical Museum. Bear left, pass through gate in fence, and reach tollgate of Bear Mountain Bridge (end of section). To continue, turn right, and cross bridge (see New York Section Nine).

Arden Valley Road (Tiorati Circle) to N.Y. 17 (Arden)
New York Section Eleven
5.5 Miles

Brief Description of Section

This section passes through Harriman State Park (see New York Section Ten for the park's history). The area in this section is filled with abandoned shafts, pits, and dumps of old iron mines, some of which date back to 1730. Tens of thousands of tons of magnetite ore were conveyed by oxen and horse teams over considerable distances to be smelted in the Greenwood Ironworks at Arden, which consisted of the Greenwood charcoal furnace built in 1811 by James Cunningham and the Clove anthracite furnace erected in 1854 by Robert and Peter Parrott. The pig iron was shipped by rail to Cornwall-on-Hudson, where it was ferried across the river to the West Point foundry at Cold Spring. There, it was made into the famous Parrott guns and shells, designed by the same brothers who operated the mines and furnaces. The Trail passes the Greenwood Mine along Surebridge Mine Road, which also leads to the Surebridge Mine and the Pine Swamp Mine south of the Trail.

Between 1861 and 1865, Arden was a booming mining town, with a population of more than 2,000 engaged primarily in mining and smelting iron ore and producing charcoal used in smelting. Smelting with coal soon replaced smelting with charcoal, and the iron deposits of Pennsylvania and the Great Lakes region were much easier to mine (although not of as high a quality). By 1890, the mining industry in this area had all but disappeared.

In earlier times, this area was inhabited by many different tribes of Indians, most recently by the Algonquins. The hiker will find many Indian names. Ramapo means "formed of round ponds," used to denote a river in which potholes occur. Tuxedo is a word that may have been derived from P'tauk-seet-tough, which means "the place of bears," though it may have come instead from Duck Cedar, a name found on old maps of the area. Scattered throughout the park are lakes with Indian names, although these lakes are, in fact, man-made and have no connection with the tribes that once inhabited the Hudson Highlands. Lake Tiorati, just east of this section of the Trail, means "sky-like." This lake formerly consisted of two bodies of water, Cedar Pond and Little Cedar Pond, which were first dammed in 1767 by Peter Hasenclever to provide a power source for his mines. One hundred-fifty years later, the ponds were again dammed, forming the present Lake Tiorati.

The route of the Trail in this section has an interesting history. The original route of the Trail—first constructed in 1922-23—remained essentially the same for many years. From Arden Valley Road, the Trail proceeded east over Green Pond Mountain, then followed along the northern shore of Island Pond and climbed to the Lemon Squeezer. However, in the late 1970s, Island Pond became a favorite location for parties, and the northern end of the lake became littered and unsightly. As a result, a shelter formerly located at Island Pond was removed, and a relocation was devised that routed the Trail around the southern end of the lake. Because of extensive wetlands at the southern end, this relocation length-ened the Trail by about two miles. In addition, the relocation eliminated all views of the lake and was considered boring by most hikers. In the meantime, conditions at the northern end of the lake improved. In 1993, the local A.T. management committee decided to restore the original route around the northern end, with some modifications to avoid steep sections. While the original route went along the lake shore, the 1993 route stays a short distance inland.

The elevation of the Trail at Arden Valley Road at the northern end of the section is 1,196 feet, and, at N.Y. 17, it is 565 feet. The highest point on this section is 1,328 feet, at the summit of Finger-board Mountain.

During very dry periods, trails in the park may be closed to the public to prevent forest fires; however, the A.T. may remain open. During such periods, hikers are advised to consult staff members at the stone building just east of N.Y. 17 on Arden Valley Road or at the stone building at the Tiorati Circle for current information as to the status of the trails in the park.

For descriptions of the various trails crossing the A.T. in this section, as well as other trails in the vicinity, consult *Harriman Trails: A Guide and History*, published by the New York-New Jersey Trail Conference.

Road Approaches

Both the northern and southern ends of this section are accessible by vehicle. At the northern end, the Trail crosses Arden Valley Road 0.3 mile west of its intersection with Seven Lakes Drive at the Tiorati Circle. No parking is available at the Trail crossing; however, ample parking is available at the Tiorati Circle (fee charged in season). At the southern end, the Trail crosses N.Y. 17 at its junction with Arden Valley Road, 0.7 mile south of Arden. No parking is available at the Trail crossing; however, ample parking is available at the Elk Pen parking area, 0.3 mile east of N.Y. 17 along Arden Valley Road.

Public Transportation

The southern end of this section can be reached from New York City and local points to the north by Short Line Bus System, (201) 529-3666. A flag stop will be made on request at the junction of N.Y. 17 and Arden Valley Road. Scheduled stops are made at the Red Apple Rest in Southfields, 2.1 miles to the south on N.Y. 17. No public transportation is available at the northern end of this section.

Maps

For route navigation, refer to Map Three with this guide. (It should be noted that the 1994 Island Pond relocation is not shown on the 1993 edition of Map Three.) For area detail, refer to the following USGS 7½-minute topographic quadrangles: Popolopen Lake and Monroe, New York. Another reference is NY-NJ TC Trail Map No. 4 (Harriman Park-North Half).

Shelters and Campsites

This section has one shelter:
Fingerboard Shelter: Stone structure built in 1928; 1.1 miles from northern end of section; 4.4 miles from southern end of section; accommodates 8; water from Lake Tiorati (0.5 mile to the east on blue-blazed Hurst Trail) or from a water faucet (summer only) at

the Tiorati Circle (0.3 mile east of A.T. crossing of Arden Valley Road; 1.4 miles north of shelter).

Next shelter: north 5.3 miles (William Brien Memorial Shelter); south 14.3 miles (Wildcat Shelter).

Supplies and Services

At the northern end of the section, refreshments may be obtained during the summer at the Tiorati Circle, 0.3 mile east of the Trail crossing of Arden Valley Road. A ranger station, bathing beach, and a public telephone are located at the Tiorati Circle. Water is available from early May until November 1 from a faucet at the northeast corner of the circle.

At the southern end, meals may be obtained at the Red Apple Rest in Southfields, 2.1 miles south of the Trail crossing on N.Y. 17. A deli, with a limited selection of groceries, is 1.8 miles south of the Trail crossing. The nearest post office is at Arden (ZIP Code 10910), 0.7 mile north of the Trail crossing. (Post office is located in former Arden railroad station, 0.2 mile east of N.Y. 17 on secondary road.) A post office is also at Southfields (ZIP Code 10975). A larger selection of groceries is in Tuxedo, 5.7 miles to the south on N.Y. 17. A public telephone is located at the Trail crossing of N.Y. 17.

Public Accommodations

At the southern end of this section, a motel is located in Southfields, 2.1 miles south of the Trail crossing on N.Y. 17.

Trail Description, North to South

Miles   **Data**

0.0   From the crest of the hill on Arden Valley Road, turn south onto woods road. In another 200 feet, the red-on-white-blazed Ramapo-Dunderberg (R-D) Trail joins the A.T. from the left, and both trails run concurrently for the next 1.2 miles.

0.1   Pass round water tank to left, cross under telephone wires, and ascend into woods on footpath.

0.5   Reach summit of Fingerboard Mountain (1,328 feet), marked by stone fireplace to right of Trail. Descend gradually, then ascend slightly, following ridge of Fingerboard Mountain.

1.1   Blue-blazed Hurst Trail on left leads in 350 feet to **Fingerboard Shelter**, visible immediately below, and, in 0.5 mile, to Seven Lakes Drive at south end of Lake Tiorati. This trail was named for Haven Hurst, a member of the Green Mountain Club, who opened the trail in 1922.

1.2   A.T. turns sharp right and begins to descend, steeply in places, as R-D Trail continues straight ahead.

1.7   At base of steep descent through hemlocks, turn left, and follow Surebridge Mine Road along Surebridge Brook, passing Greenwood Mine, now a water-filled pit, to left of Trail. During the Civil War, iron from this mine was transported to the Greenwood Furnace in Arden.

1.8   Turn right, and cross Surebridge Brook. Begin ascent of Surebridge Mountain.

2.1   Reach height of land on Surebridge Mountain, and begin to descend.

2.4   After steep descent, turn left, and follow left bank of intermittent stream, then cross stream, and continue along right side of stream.

2.5   Turn right, leaving stream.

2.6   Cross turquoise-blazed Long Path.

2.7   Turn left, and begin ascent of Island Pond Mountain.

3.0   Reach summit of Island Pond Mountain (1,303 feet), and turn left as Arden-Surebridge (A-SB) Trail, with red-triangle-on-white blazes, comes in from right and joins A.T. Trail begins gradual descent.

3.2   Reach top of Lemon Squeezer, a narrow, steep passage between boulders. Descend very steeply. If descent is too steep, use bypass trail to the right. At bottom of Lemon Squeezer, A-SB Trail makes sharp left, while A.T. bears right and ascends briefly.

3.4   Begin to descend.

3.5   Turn right on the Crooked Road, an old woods road. In another 300 feet, cross the inlet of Island Pond, and immediately turn left, leaving the Crooked Road.

3.7   After ascent, reach crest of rise, with view of Island Pond to left, and begin to descend.

3.8   Cross bridge over outlet of Island Pond. The outlet is partially channeled into a spillway made of cut stones. This spillway was constructed by the CCC in 1934, as part of a plan to dam the pond and thereby enlarge it. However, the work was never completed, and the pond remains in its natural state. The A.T. now bears left and starts to climb.

3.9   Cross gravel road, which provides automobile access for fishermen to Island Pond (by permit only). (To right, the gravel road leads in 0.3 mile to Arden Valley Road.) In another 250 feet, turn left onto Island Pond Road, a woods road, built by Edward Harriman around 1905.

4.0   Turn right, leaving Island Pond Road, and begin to ascend Green Pond Mountain.

4.1   Turn sharply right at point of switchback, and continue to ascend.

4.2   Reach summit of Green Pond Mountain, and turn left, continuing along summit ridge.

4.4   Turn left, and begin to descend on long switchback. Straight ahead, open rocks offer view to west.

4.5   Turn sharply right at point of switchback, and continue to descend.

4.6   Descend steeply on short switchbacks, then level off, soon resuming gradual descent.

4.9   With paved road visible to right, bear left, and continue to descend.

5.0   Turn right on Old Arden Road (woods road that once connected the Arden estate of the Harriman family with Tuxedo, now partially destroyed by the construction of the N.Y. State Thruway). Skirt the Elk Pen Field to the left. This field, with pieces of metal fence, is all that remains of an unsuccessful attempt by the Harrimans to establish an elk herd here.

5.1   Reach paved Arden Valley Road. Turn left, and follow road. Arden-Surebridge (A-SB) Trail (red-triangle-on-white blazes) runs concurrently with A.T. along road.

5.2   Pass entrance to Elk Pen parking area on left.

5.3	Cross N.Y. State Thruway and railroad tracks on overpass, and continue along road, passing stone building (ranger's house) to left.
5.5	Reach N.Y. 17 (end of section). To continue, cross road, and reenter woods (see New York Section Twelve).

Trail Description, South to North

Miles   **Data**

0.0	From N.Y. 17, proceed east on paved Arden Valley Road.
0.2	Cross railroad tracks and N.Y. State Thruway on overpass. At this point, the A.T. runs concurrently with the Arden-Surebridge (A-SB) Trail (red-triangle-on-white blazes).
0.3	Pass entrance to Elk Pen parking area on right.
0.4	Turn right on chained-off woods road (Old Arden Road), skirting the Elk Pen Field to the right. A-SB Trail continues ahead on paved road. Old Arden Road at one time connected the Arden estate of the Harriman family with Tuxedo but was partially destroyed by construction of N.Y. State Thruway. Broken metal fence around field is all that remains of the Harrimans' unsuccessful attempt to establish an elk herd here.
0.5	Turn left, leaving Old Arden Road, and begin to ascend Green Pond Mountain.
0.6	With paved road visible to left, bear slightly right, and continue to ascend.
0.8	Trail levels off briefly, then resumes steeper ascent on switchbacks.
1.0	With steep rocks straight ahead, turn right, and ascend on graded trail, then bear sharply left at switchback.
1.1	Reach summit of Green Pond Mountain, and turn right, continuing along summit ridge. Open rocks straight ahead offer views to west.
1.3	Turn right, and begin to descend.
1.4	Turn sharply left at point of switchback, and continue to descend.

1.5   Reach base of descent, and turn left onto Island Pond Road, a woods road that runs along the western shore of Island Pond. This road was built by Edward Harriman around 1905.

1.6   Turn right, leaving Island Pond Road, and soon climb log steps. In another 250 feet, cross gravel road, which provides automobile access for fishermen to Island Pond (by permit only), and begin to descend. (To left, the gravel road leads in 0.3 mile to Arden Valley Road.)

1.7   Bear right, and cross bridge over outlet of Island Pond. The outlet is partially channeled into a spillway made of cut stones. This spillway was constructed by the CCC in 1934, as part of a plan to dam the pond and thereby enlarge it. However, the work was never completed, and the pond remains in its natural state. The A.T. now starts to climb.

1.8   Reach crest of rise, with view of Island Pond to right, and begin to descend.

2.0   Turn right onto the Crooked Road, an old woods road, and immediately cross the inlet of Island Pond. In another 300 feet, turn left, leaving the Crooked Road, and soon begin to ascend.

2.2   After a brief descent, reach the Lemon Squeezer, a narrow, steep passage between large boulders. The Arden-Surebridge (A-SB) Trail, with red-triangle-on-white blazes, comes in from right, and both trails climb together through this formation, approximately 300 feet to the top. If climb is too steep, use bypass trail to left. From top of Lemon Squeezer, Trail ascends gradually up Island Pond Mountain.

2.5   Reach summit of Island Pond Mountain (1,303 feet). Trail turns right and begins to descend. (A-SB Trail continues straight ahead, and reaches Arden Valley Road in about 0.4 mile.)

2.9   Cross turquoise-blazed Long Path.

3.0   Turn left, following left bank of intermittent stream, then cross stream, and continue along right bank of stream.

3.1   Turn right, leaving stream, and ascend steeply.

3.4   Reach height of land on Surebridge Mountain, and begin to descend.

3.7   Cross Surebridge Brook, and turn left onto Surebridge Mine Road. Pass Greenwood Mine to right of Trail, now a water-filled pit. During the Civil War, iron ore from this mine was transported to the Greenwood Furnace in Arden.

3.8   Turn right, and begin steep ascent through hemlocks.

4.3   Reach ridge of Fingerboard Mountain, and turn left as red-on-white-blazed Ramapo-Dunderberg (R-D) Trail comes in from right and joins A.T.

4.4   Blue-blazed Hurst Trail on right leads in 350 feet to **Fingerboard Shelter**, immediately visible below, and in 0.5 mile to Seven Lakes Drive at south end of Lake Tiorati. This trail was named for Haven Hurst, a member of the Green Mountain Club, who opened it in 1922.

5.0   Reach summit of Fingerboard Mountain (1,328 feet), marked by stone fireplace to left of Trail. Begin to descend.

5.4   Pass under telephone wires, and join woods road, with round water tank to right.

5.5   Reach paved Arden Valley Road (end of section). In another 300 feet, the R-D Trail leaves to the right. To continue, cross road and follow Trail north into woods (see New York Section Ten).

N.Y. 17 (Arden) to N.Y. 17A (Mt. Peter)
New York Section Twelve
12.0 Miles

Brief Description of Section

This section of the A.T. traverses four mountains—Arden Mountain, Buchanan Mountain, Mombasha High Point, and Bellvale Mountain. It runs through the northern section of Sterling Forest, a 20,000-acre tract that was once owned by the Harriman family. Included in its boundaries are the sites of many former iron mines and of the Sterling Furnace, which supplied the famous chain which stretched across the Hudson River near West Point, during the Revolutionary War.

Hikers on this section of the Trail may notice interesting circular depressions on the forest floor. These are the remains of burning pits where wood was converted to charcoal, needed for the smelting of iron ore. During the 1800s, the hills in this area were virtually denuded of vegetation as a result of harvesting the timber needed to produce the charcoal. The forest the hiker sees today is mostly secondary growth. Brooks and streams in the area are often colored brown as a result of iron salts leaching through the soil.

Sterling Forest is named for Lord Stirling, a Revolutionary War general of Scottish origin, who fought in the battle of Long Island and other battles but died at Albany from natural causes before the war ended. Lord Stirling, whose original name was William Alexander, claimed the title of Earl of Stirling, although he never officially received the title. His father, James Alexander, surveyed land around the New York-New Jersey boundary and bought various parcels of land that contained iron and other minerals.

The Harriman family bought Sterling Forest in the late 1800s and offered the land to New York State for park purposes in the early 1950s. Unfortunately, the state declined at that time to acquire the property, claiming that it contained too many wetlands and other problem areas and asserting that New York already had sufficient parklands to provide for future needs. As a result, the Harriman family sold the land to private interests. During the 1970s, the

National Park Service acquired the narrow corridor through which the Trail presently runs.

In the mid-1980s, the new owners of Sterling Forest announced plans to develop it, and concerned citizens began extensive efforts to preserve the property in its natural state. As a result, Passaic County, New Jersey, acquired by condemnation the 2,100 acres of Sterling Forest located in New Jersey. The National Park Service also acquired additional lands to buffer the A.T. around Little Dam Lake. The New York-New Jersey Trail Conference and many other environmental organizations have joined with the Palisades Interstate Park Commission and the states of New York and New Jersey to form the Public/Private Partnership to Save Sterling Forest, which is working to preserve the remainder of this important natural resource.

As of this writing (1994), negotiations are still underway with the owners of Sterling Forest. It is hoped that this beautiful piece of land, which is a viewshed for the A.T., will soon be permanently preserved for the benefit of present and future generations.

The elevation at N.Y. 17 is 500 feet; at N.Y. 17A, the elevation is 1,130 feet. The highest elevation is 1,294 feet, on Bellvale Mountain.

Road Approaches

Both the northern and southern ends of this section are accessible by vehicle. At the northern end, the Trail crosses N.Y. 17 at its junction with Arden Valley Road, 0.7 mile south of Arden. No parking is available at the Trail crossing; however, ample parking is available at the Elk Pen parking area on Arden Valley Road, 0.3 mile east of its intersection with N.Y. 17. Drivers approaching this end of the Trail via the New York Thruway should note that the closest exits onto N.Y. 17 are at Harriman to the north (exit 16) and Suffern to the south (exit 15).

At the southern end, the Trail crosses N.Y. 17A at Mt. Peter, two miles north of the village of Greenwood Lake and 1.6 miles east of Bellvale. Parking is available on the paved strip of the old highway (known as Continental Road) around which the improved N.Y. 17A has been built.

Road access is also available at Orange Turnpike (1.8 miles from the northern end of the section), East Mombasha Road (3.2 miles from the northern end of the section), West Mombasha Road (4.9 miles from the northern end of the section), and Lakes Road (3.6 miles from the southern end of the section). No parking is available at Orange Turnpike or West Mombasha Road. Limited parking is available at East Mombasha Road and Lakes Road, but overnight parking is not permitted.

Public Transportation

The northern end of this section can be reached from New York City and local points to the north by Short Line Bus System, (201) 529-3666. A flag stop will be made on request at the Trail crossing at Arden Valley Road, and scheduled stops are made at the Red Apple Rest in Southfields, 2.1 miles south of the A.T. on N.Y. 17.

The southern end of this section can be reached from New York City and from Warwick, New York, by New Jersey Transit buses (Route No. 196-197), (201) 762-5100. A flag stop will be made on request at Mt. Peter (Kain Road), 0.2 mile west of the A.T. on N.Y. 17A.

Maps

For route navigation, refer to Map Three with this guide. For area detail, refer to the following USGS 7½-minute topographic quadrangles: Monroe, New York; Warwick, New York; Greenwood Lake, New York-New Jersey.

Shelters and Campsites

This section has one shelter:

Wildcat Shelter: Built in 1992 by local volunteers; 9.9 miles from northern end of section; 2.1 miles from southern end of section; accommodates 8; well with hand pump, privy, cast-iron fire ring, and three tent sites also available. The pump is operational from April to November only; at other times, water may be obtained from a spring.

Next shelter: north 14.3 miles (Fingerboard Shelter); south 12.0 miles (Wawayanda Shelter).

Supplies and Services

At the northern end of this section, meals may be obtained at the Red Apple Rest in Southfields, 2.1 miles south of the A.T. on N.Y. 17. A deli, with a limited selection of groceries, is 1.8 miles south of the Trail crossing. The nearest post office is at Arden (ZIP Code 10910), 0.7 mile north of the A.T. on N.Y. 17. (Post office is located in the former Arden railroad station, 0.2 mile east of N.Y. 17 on secondary road.) A post office is at Southfields (ZIP Code 10975), too. A larger selection of groceries is available in Tuxedo, 5.5 miles to the south on N.Y. 17. A public telephone is located at the Trail crossing of N.Y. 17.

The southern end has a grocery store and post office (ZIP Code 10912) at Bellvale, 1.6 miles west of the A.T. on N.Y. 17A. A variety of supplies and services, including restaurants, a supermarket, and a post office (ZIP Code 10925), is available at Greenwood Lake, 2.0 miles south of the A.T. on N.Y. 17A and N.Y. 210.

Public Accommodations

The northern end of this section has a motel at Southfields, 2.1 miles south of the A.T. on N.Y. 17. At the southern end, tourist homes are available in Greenwood Lake, 2.0 miles south of the A.T. on N.Y. 17A and N.Y. 210, and motels are available in Warwick, 3.5 miles to the west along N.Y. 17A.

Trail Description, North to South

Miles   **Data**

0.0   From west side of N.Y. 17 at Arden Valley Road, proceed west, entering woods on footpath. Soon begin steep (very steep in places) climb of Agony Grind.

0.4   Reach viewpoint to east over Ramapo Valley and N.Y. State Thruway, with Harriman State Park beyond. Grade moderates.

0.8   Please sign Trail register located on tree to left of Trail.

0.9   Reach brush-covered area, with limited view back over Ramapo Valley to Harriman State Park, then descend briefly.

1.1   Reach scrub oak-covered summit of Arden Mountain (1,180 feet), with limited views west and north. Trail descends through hemlock grove.

1.5   After brief ascent, reach secondary peak, with views to west. Begin to descend.

1.6   Rocky ledges allow views west to Mombasha High Point and Bellvale Mountain and north to Catskill Mountains on the horizon. Trail continues to descend.

1.8   Reach paved Orange Turnpike. A pipe spring, a water source, is 0.5 mile south of Trail crossing on east side of road, by a gravel pull-off area beyond a dip in road. Trail turns left along road for 250 feet, crosses road, and reenters woods, climbing steeply through hemlocks.

2.0   Trail levels off.

2.1   At viewpoint to left, turn right, and begin to descend through hemlock grove.

2.2   Trail levels off.

2.5   Reach eastern end of Little Dam Lake. Trail passes around northern side of lake, which is visible to left of Trail.

2.9   Cross wood-truss bridge over inlet of Little Dam Lake.

3.0   Trail continues on old, winding woods road.

3.2   Reach paved East Mombasha Road. Cross road, and reenter woods on footpath, ascending steadily.

3.4   Reach viewpoint to east over Little Dam Lake at secondary summit of Buchanan Mountain, then steeply descend rocky, hemlock-covered slope.

3.5   Cross stream.

3.6   Cross second stream.

3.7   After descent, cross third stream. In 200 feet, cross fourth stream, and begin steady ascent.

4.0   Reach beautiful viewpoint near summit of Buchanan Mountain (1,142 feet).

4.2   Trail runs along edge of escarpment.

4.3   Turn left, and descend steeply over jumbled rocks.

4.5   After passing through hemlock grove and mountain-laurel thicket, cross stream, and ascend briefly.

4.7   Turn right, and descend rocky slope.

4.8   Cross stream.
4.9   Reach paved West Mombasha Road. Turn left, and follow road.
5.0   Turn right, cross road, cross bridge over ditch, and follow posts across field.
5.1   Reach end of field, and continue on old woods road.
5.3   Ascend steeply, then turn left at top of ascent.
5.5   Cross grassy woods road, and continue to ascend.
5.7   Turn left onto dirt road, and pass through gap in stone wall. Continue straight ahead on footpath as dirt road curves to right. Trail ascends gradually.
6.1   After ascent on switchbacks, reach Mombasha High Point (1,280 feet). Mombasha Lake is visible below (to left), with Schunemunk Mountain behind to the northeast. Kloiber's Pond is straight ahead (along road). Harriman State Park is visible to the east, and, on a clear day, New York City may be seen on the horizon, due magnetic south. To the west is the ridge of Bellvale Mountain.
6.9   Blue-blazed Allis Trail branches off to left and descends over One Cedar Mountain to N.Y. 17A. This trail is named for banker J. Ashton Allis, a pioneer trail builder, for many years president of Fresh Air Club, and an early treasurer of ATC. A viewpoint is located 100 feet down Allis Trail, with High Point Monument and relay towers and Mt. Tammany at Delaware Water Gap visible to west. A.T. makes sharp right turn and descends.
7.0   Trail levels off.
7.1   Make sharp right turn.
7.7   Pass old stone walls, remains of an abandoned settlement, to right of Trail.
7.9   Cross dirt road, then cross tributary stream.
8.0   Cross a tributary of Trout Brook, then cross the brook.
8.1   Reach top of Fitzgerald Falls, a 25-foot waterfall in a rocky cleft. Turn left, and steeply descend on rock steps along left side of falls. At base of falls, turn right, crossing the brook, and continue along the brook. Blue-blazed bypass trail, which passes straight ahead through hemlock grove, avoids two crossings of brook and frequently flooded area and rejoins A.T. in 0.1 mile.

8.4   Cross wooden bridge over Trout Brook, and follow Trail uphill to paved Lakes Road (Monroe Road). Cross road, reenter woods, and soon begin to ascend Bellvale Mountain.

8.8   After steep ascent, make sharp left turn, and ascend more gradually.

9.0   Turn left onto old woods road (now merely a footpath), and continue to ascend gradually.

9.5   Trail levels off, then begins to descend.

9.7   Cross old stone wall.

9.9   Blue-blazed trail to right leads 600 feet to **Wildcat Shelter**, with spring, well, and hand pump. In 225 feet, after junction of A.T. with side trail to shelter, cross small brook.

10.2   Climb to top of Cat Rocks, an upturned strata of reddish conglomerate (puddingstone), with top leveled by glacial action. Views to the east and south. Blue-blazed trail bypasses steep climb and rejoins A.T. in 275 feet.

10.4   Cross brook.

10.6   Leave woods, and cross rocky area.

10.7   Reach top of Eastern Pinnacles, another conglomerate outcropping, with good views north, east, and south over Greenwood Lake. Blue-blazed trail to right bypasses steep descent and rejoins A.T. in 150 feet. Descend steeply from rocks and continue along grassy road, soon beginning gradual ascent.

10.9   Trail levels off.

11.3   Cross cleared utility right-of-way.

11.6   Continue on footpath as woods road curves off to right.

12.0   Reach N.Y. 17A. Turn right, and follow road for 150 feet, then take left fork onto old road (Continental Road). Continue on Continental Road for 150 feet until Trail turns left and reenters woods on footpath end of section (see New York Section Thirteen).

Trail Description, South to North

Miles   Data

0.0   Proceed east along Continental Road for 150 feet to its intersection with N.Y. 17A, then cross to northern side of

N.Y. 17A. Turn right, and follow road for 150 feet, then turn left, and enter woods on footpath.

0.4 Join woods road coming in from left, and continue on woods road.

0.7 Cross cleared utility right-of-way.

1.1 Trail begins to descend gradually.

1.3 Climb steeply to top of Eastern Pinnacles, an upturned strata of reddish conglomerate (puddingstone), with good views north, east, and south over Greenwood Lake Valley. Blue-blazed trail bypasses steep climb and rejoins A.T. in 150 feet.

1.6 Cross brook.

1.8 Climb to top of Cat Rocks, another conglomerate outcropping with top leveled by glacial action. Views to the east and south. Blue-blazed trail to right bypasses steep climb and rejoins A.T. in 275 feet.

2.1 Cross small brook. In another 225 feet, blue-blazed trail to left leads 600 feet to **Wildcat Shelter**, with spring, well, and hand pump. Trail begins to ascend.

2.3 Cross old stone wall. Trail continues to ascend.

2.5 Trail levels off, then descends gradually.

3.0 Turn right, ascend briefly, then continue to descend.

3.2 Make sharp right turn at double blaze, and begin steeper descent.

3.6 Reach paved Lakes Road (Monroe Road). Cross road, descend on footpath, and cross wooden bridge over Trout Brook.

3.8 Cross brook , then turn left, and continue along brook through hemlock grove. Blue-blazed bypass trail bears right and ascends through hemlocks, avoiding two additional crossings of brook and area that is frequently flooded. Bypass trail rejoins A.T. in 0.1 mile at base of falls.

3.9 Reach base of Fitzgerald Falls, a 25-foot waterfall in a rocky cleft. Cross stream just below falls, and ascend steeply on rock steps along right side of falls.

4.0 Cross stream and tributary stream, and pass through hemlock grove.

4.1 Cross tributary stream again, then cross dirt road, and continue to ascend.

4.3   Pass stone walls, remains of an abandoned settlement, to left of Trail.

4.9   Make sharp left turn.

5.0   Begin steady ascent.

5.1   At top of rise, blue-blazed Allis Trail branches off to right and descends over One Cedar Mountain to N.Y. 17A. This trail is named for banker J. Ashton Allis, a pioneer trail builder, for many years president of Fresh Air Club, and an early treasurer of ATC. A viewpoint is located 100 feet down Allis Trail, with High Point Monument, relay towers, and Mt. Tammany at Delaware Water Gap visible to west. A.T. levels off.

5.9   Reach Mombasha High Point (1,280 feet). Mombasha Lake is visible below (to left), with Schunemunk Mountain behind it to the northeast. Kloiber's Pond is straight ahead (along road). Harriman State Park is visible to the east, and, on a clear day, New York City may be seen on the horizon, due magnetic south. To the west is the ridge of Bellvale Mountain. Trail descends on switchbacks.

6.3   Join dirt road that comes in from left. In another 100 feet, pass through gap in stone wall, then turn right, leave dirt road, and continue on footpath.

6.5   After descent, cross grassy woods road.

6.7   Turn right, descend steeply, and bear left on old woods road.

6.9   Emerge onto overgrown field. Follow posts across field.

7.0   Cross bridge over ditch, and reach paved West Mombasha Road. Turn left, and follow road.

7.1   Turn right, cross road, and reenter woods.

7.2   Cross stream. In 200 feet, turn left, ascending rocky slope.

7.5   After brief descent, cross stream, then pass through mountain-laurel thicket and hemlock grove.

7.7   Ascend steeply over jumbled rocks, then turn right, and follow edge of escarpment.

8.0   Reach viewpoint near summit of Buchanan Mountain (1,142 feet). Begin steady descent.

8.3   Cross stream. In 200 feet, cross second stream, and ascend.

8.4   Cross third stream.

8.5   Cross fourth stream, then steeply ascend rocky slope.

8.6   Reach second summit of Buchanan Mountain, with view to east over Little Dam Lake. Begin to descend.

8.8   Reach paved East Mombasha Road. Cross road, and continue on old, winding woods road.

9.0   Woods road narrows into footpath.

9.1   Cross wood-truss bridge over inlet of Little Dam Lake. Trail passes around north shore of lake, which is visible to right of Trail.

9.5   Reach east end of lake.

9.8   Begin moderately steep ascent through hemlock grove.

9.9   Turn left at top of ascent, with views to left.

10.0   Begin descent through hemlock grove.

10.2   After steeper descent, reach paved Orange Turnpike. A pipe spring, a water source, is 0.5 mile south of Trail crossing on the east side of the road, by a gravel pull-off area beyond a dip in the road. Trail turns left along road for 250 feet, then crosses road, and reenters woods, beginning ascent of Arden Mountain.

10.4   Rocky ledges allow views west to Mombasha High Point and Bellvale Mountain and north to Catskill Mountains on the horizon. Trail continues to ascend.

10.5   Reach secondary peak. Begin to descend.

10.7   Ascend steadily through hemlock grove.

10.9   Reach scrub oak-covered summit of Arden Mountain (1,180 feet), with limited views west and north.

11.1   After brief ascent, reach brush-covered area.

11.2   Please sign the Trail register located on tree to right of Trail.

11.6   At viewpoint to east over Ramapo Valley and N.Y. State Thruway, with Harriman State Park beyond, begin steep (very steep in places) descent of Agony Grind.

12.0   Reach N.Y. 17 at its intersection with Arden Valley Road (end of section). To continue, cross N.Y. 17, and continue east on Arden Valley Road (see New York Section Eleven).

N.Y. 17A (Mt. Peter) to
New York-New Jersey State Line
New York Section Thirteen
5.9 Miles

Brief Description of Section

The Trail in this section follows the ridge of Bellvale Mountain, with many beautiful views over Greenwood Lake and the Ramapo Hills from open ledges. Although the elevation changes little from the northern end of the section at N.Y. 17A (1,130 feet) to the southern end at the state line (about 1,350 feet), the route has many short, steep ascents and descents along the crest of the ridge. The highest point is at Prospect Rock (1,433 feet). Several unmarked side trails descend from the A.T. to N.Y. 210. Except for the State Line Trail (see page 119), these trails are not officially maintained and, in fact, cross private property. The Trail passes through oak and hickory forests, with pitch pine on the rocky ledges.

Road Approaches

At the northern end of the section, the Trail crosses N.Y. 17A at Mt. Peter, two miles north of the village of Greenwood Lake and 1.6 miles east of Bellvale. This end of the section starts at Continental Road, the paved strip of the old highway around which improved N.Y. 17A has been built. Ample parking is available along Continental Road at the Trail crossing.

The southern end of the section is at the New York-New Jersey state boundary. The nearest road access to this point is from N.Y. 210, which runs along the shore of Greenwood Lake. The State Line Trail (see description at end of section) ascends from opposite the Greenwood Lake Marina on N.Y. 210 and follows the state line for 1.2 miles until it reaches the A.T. on the crest of Bellvale Mountain. Parking for two to three cars may be available at the intersection of N.Y. 210 with Lake Shore Drive, immediately north of the Greenwood Lake Marina. Parking is not permitted at the marina.

Public Transportation

Both ends of this section can be reached from New York City and from Warwick, New York, by New Jersey Transit buses (Route No. 196-197, (201) 762-5100). At the northern end, a flag stop will be made on request at Mt. Peter (Kain Road), 0.2 mile west of the Trail crossing on N.Y. 17A. A flag stop also will be made at the junction of the State Line Trail and N.Y. 210 at the Greenwood Lake Marina, 1.2 miles from the southern end of the section via the State Line Trail.

Maps

For route navigation, refer to Maps Three and Four with this guide. For area detail, refer to the following USGS 7½-minute topographic quadrangle: Greenwood Lake, New York-New Jersey. Another reference is NY-NJ TC North Jersey Trails Map No. 21.

Shelters and Campsites

No shelters or campsites are available in this section.

Supplies and Services

The northern end of this section has a grocery store and post office (ZIP Code 10912) at Bellvale, 1.6 miles west of the A.T. on N.Y. 17A. A wide variety of supplies and services, including restaurants, a supermarket, and a post office (ZIP Code 10925), is available in the village of Greenwood Lake. From the northern end of the section, Greenwood Lake is two miles to the south via N.Y. 17A and 210. At the southern end of the section, meals may be obtained at the Lakeside Inn, 1.1 miles south of the terminus of the State Line Trail on County 511 (the continuation in New Jersey of N.Y. 210).

Public Accommodations

Tourist homes are located in Greenwood Lake, two miles south of the northern end of this section, and motels are available in Warwick, 3.5 miles to the west, along N.Y. 17A. A motel is located on County 511 (the continuation in New Jersey of N.Y. 210), 1.8 miles south of the terminus of the State Line Trail.

Trail Description, North to South

Miles   **Data**

0.0   From paved Continental Road, turn south, and enter woods. Cross woods road, and ascend.

0.5   At powerline clearing, there are good views to the east.

0.8   Under telephone lines, cross brook, which is the outlet of marsh to right of Trail.

1.8   Unmarked and unmaintained trail leads to the left.

2.0   Water symbol on tree indicates the start of unmarked, unmaintained trail that descends to right. Spring is to the left of the trail on private property, 225 yards downhill.

2.2   Emerge onto an exposed section of the ridge, with beautiful views of Greenwood Lake to the east. Originally known as Long Pond, Greenwood Lake was dammed to increase its size, first in the 1760s and again in the early 1800s, when it served as a water source for the Morris Canal.

2.5   Descend steeply, and cross small brook.

2.9   After passing through clearing, cross Cascade Brook, and ascend through hemlocks.

3.1   Trail ascends to viewpoint.

3.3   Descend to brook in hollow, then ascend, crossing brook several times.

3.4   Emerge again onto open rocks, with good views to the east over Greenwood Lake. Ascend briefly, then come out once more on exposed rocks, with more views.

3.9   Reach rock outcrop with 360-degree view. Continue along open rocks on east side of ridge, with views of Greenwood Lake below.

4.3   Descend very steeply, then cross old road, and turn left.

4.5   Cross Furnace Brook, a water source.

4.9   Begin gradual ascent.

5.3   After steep climb, take sharp left. To right, rocky promontory provides beautiful western, northern, and eastern views. In another 150 feet, turn left again.

5.4 Reach Prospect Rock (1,433 feet), with magnificent views over Greenwood Lake to the east and Taylor and Warwick mountains to the west.

5.6 Please sign Trail register located on pine tree to left of Trail.

5.7 Beautiful views to west from open rocks.

5.9 Reach blue-blazed State Line Trail at New York-New Jersey state line (end of section). (See page 119 for description of this trail.) To continue, proceed straight ahead (see New Jersey Section One).

Trail Description, South to North

Miles   Data

0.0 From intersection of blue-blazed State Line Trail at New Jersey-New York state line, proceed north on footpath.

0.1 Beautiful western views from open rocks.

0.3 Please sign Trail register located on pine tree to right of Trail.

0.5 After short climb, reach Prospect Rock (1,433 feet). Magnificent eastern views over Greenwood Lake and Taylor mountains to the west.

0.6 Turn right, and cross to east side of ridge. In another 150 feet, take sharp right, and descend, first steeply, then more gradually. Before second turn, rocky promontory directly ahead provides beautiful views to the west, north, and east.

1.3 Cross Furnace Brook, a source of water.

1.6 After crossing old road, climb steeply, then very steeply, and reach viewpoints to the south, east, and west. Trail follows crest of the ridge for next 0.4 mile, with many good views of Greenwood Lake below.

2.4 Trail again comes out on open rocks, with good eastern views over Greenwood Lake. Descend briefly, then come out once more on exposed rocks, with more views.

2.5 Take sharp left, and begin to descend, crossing small brook several times; then, ascend gradually.

2.8 Trail begins to descend.

3.0   After descending through hemlocks, cross Cascade Brook, and pass through clearing; then ascend briefly.

3.4   Cross small brook, then, ascend steeply.

3.5   Reach viewpoint over Greenwood Lake. Originally known as Long Pond, Greenwood Lake was dammed to increase its size, first in the 1760s and then again in the early 1800s, when it served as a water source for the Morris Canal. Continue along ridge, with additional views of the lake below.

3.7   Turn left, away from exposed ridge, and enter woods on grassy footpath.

3.9   Water symbol on tree indicates the start of unmarked, unmaintained trail that descends to left. Spring is on private property to the left of trail, 225 yards downhill.

4.1   Unmarked, unmaintained trail leads to right.

5.1   Cross brook under telephone lines; the brook is the outlet of the marsh to the left of the Trail.

5.4   At clearing for powerlines, there are good eastern views.

5.9   Reach paved Continental Road (end of section). To continue, turn right along road, and proceed along N.Y. 17A, which comes in from left. Then, turn left, and enter woods (see New York Section Twelve).

State Line Trail

This blue-blazed trail descends from the A.T. and follows the New York-New Jersey state line to N.Y. 210 opposite the Greenwood Lake Marina. From its junction with the A.T. at the southern end of this section, it proceeds east and crosses the ridge of Bellvale Mountain, with numerous short ascents and descents. At 0.4 mile, the Trail turns sharply to the right, then immediately to the left, and starts a steady descent. The yellow-blazed Ernest Walter Trail, which makes a loop around Surprise Lake and West Pond, turns off to the right at 0.5 mile. At 0.7 mile, log steps along the trail prevent erosion. With houses in view to the right at 0.9 mile, the Trail turns left and continues descent until it reaches N.Y. 210, opposite the Greenwood Lake Marina, at 1.2 miles.

New York-New Jersey State Line to N.J. 94
New Jersey Section One
9.6 Miles

Brief Description of Section

This section begins at the New York-New Jersey state line along the ridge of Bearfort Mountain, west of Greenwood Lake. The Trail follows the ridge for about 0.3 mile, passing through Abram S. Hewitt State Forest, then turns right and begins to run in a generally northwesterly direction. After crossing Warwick Turnpike, it traverses Wawayanda State Park. The Trail passes through an upland deciduous forest, with some red cedar, hemlock, and rhododendron.

Wawayanda is a Munsee Indian word that literally means "winding, winding water." It was applied by the local Indians to the creeks and meadows along the valleys in southern Orange County (New York) and northern Sussex County (New Jersey). Wawayanda Mountain had been named by the time of the Revolutionary War, and, in 1846, the name was given to Wawayanda Lake, which was created from two natural ponds.

Road Approaches

Only the southern end of this section is directly accessible by vehicle. The southern end is on N.J. 94, about 0.6 mile north of the intersection of N.J. 94 and Maple Grange Road, and about 2.4 miles north of Vernon. A designated parking area is at the Trail crossing.

The northern end of the section is at the New York-New Jersey state boundary. The nearest road access to this point is from N.Y. 210, which runs along the shore of Greenwood Lake. The State Line Trail (see page 119) ascends from opposite the Greenwood Lake Marina on N.Y. 210 and follows the state line for 1.2 miles until it reaches the A.T. on the crest of Bellvale Mountain. Parking for two to three cars may be available at the intersection of N.Y. 210 with Lake Shore Drive, immediately north of the Greenwood Lake Marina. Parking is not permitted at the marina.

In addition, road access is available at Long House Road (Brady Road), 2.2 miles from the northern end of the section, and at Warwick Turnpike, 3.6 miles from the northern end. No parking is available at the Trail crossings of Long House Road or Warwick Turnpike, but ample parking is available at the headquarters of Wawayanda State Park, located off Warwick Turnpike about 0.3 mile south of the Trail crossing. Registration is required for overnight parking at park headquarters. A blue-blazed side trail links the park headquarters with the A.T., 3.9 miles from the northern end of the section.

Public Transportation

The State Line Trail, leading to the northern end of this section, can be reached from New York City and Warwick, New York, by New Jersey Transit buses (Route No. 196-197, (201) 762-5100). A flag stop can be requested for the junction of the State Line Trail and N.Y. 210 at the Greenwood Lake Marina. No public transportation is available at the southern end of the section.

Maps

For route navigation, refer to Map Four with this guide. For area detail, refer to the following USGS 7½-minute topographic quadrangles: Greenwood Lake, New York-New Jersey; Wawayanda, New Jersey-New York. Another reference is NY-NJ TC North Jersey Trails Map No. 21.

Shelters and Campsites

This section has one shelter:

Wawayanda Shelter: Built in 1990 by residents of Vernon Township with assistance from staff of Wawayanda State Park; 4.0 miles from northern end of section; 5.6 miles from southern end of section; 0.1 mile from the A.T. on blue-blazed side trail; accommodates 6; water available at park headquarters, 0.4 mile from shelter (reached via another blue-blazed side trail).

Next shelter: north 12.0 miles (Wildcat Shelter); south 13.0 miles (Pochuck Mountain Shelter).

Supplies and Services

At the northern end of the section, meals may be obtained at the Lakeside Inn, 1.1 miles south of the terminus of the State Line Trail on County 511 (the continuation in New Jersey of N.Y. 210). At the southern end, a seasonal farm market is 0.1 mile to the north along N.J. 94, and a shopping center, with a 24-hour supermarket, a pizzeria, a deli, restaurants, and a post office (ZIP Code 07462), is in Vernon, 2.4 miles south of the Trail crossing along N.J. 94 and County 515. Another seasonal farm market/ice cream stand is on Warwick Turnpike, 0.2 mile south of the Trail crossing, and meals are available at restaurants along Warwick Turnpike, both 0.8 mile north and 1.5 miles south of the Trail crossing. A supermarket is at the junction of N.Y. 94 and Warwick Turnpike, 2.7 miles north of the Trail crossing of Warwick Turnpike. A deli, with groceries, is on Warwick Turnpike, 1.8 miles south of the Trail crossing. A deli and post office (Zip Code 10959) are in New Milford, New York, 1.8 miles north of the Trail crossing of Barrett Road (go north on Barrett Road for 1.6 miles, then turn right, and follow N.Y. 94 for 0.2 mile to Ryerson Road).

Public Accommodations

At the northern end of the section, a motel is located along County 511 (the continuation in New Jersey of N.Y. 210), 1.8 miles south of the terminus of the State Line Trail on N.Y. 210. At the southern end of the section, the Appalachian Motel is located along N.J. 94, 1.4 miles south of the Trail crossing. In addition, lodging may be obtained at the Willow Brook Inn, 0.8 mile north of the Trail crossing of Warwick Turnpike.

Trail Description, North to South

Miles   **Data**

0.0   From junction with State Line Trail, continue south on A.T.

0.2   Reach eastern viewpoint over Surprise Lake and Sterling Ridge, and begin to descend.

0.3   A.T. turns right as yellow-blazed Ernest Walter Trail continues straight ahead. Ernest Walter Trail makes loop around West Pond and Surprise Lake and connects in about 1.0 mile with the white-blazed Bearfort Ridge Trail, leading 2.5 miles south to Warwick Turnpike.

0.5   Reach rock ledge, with western view.

0.7   Cross rocks over small stream.

0.8   Cross woods road. In 450 feet, cross another woods road.

1.0   Turn left onto dirt road for 45 feet, then turn right, and continue to descend.

1.1   Cross split-log bridge over Long House Creek.

1.5   Cross log bridge over stream.

1.7   Turn right onto woods road for 35 feet, then turn left, and reenter woods.

1.9   Turn right onto grassy woods road.

2.0   Turn left, and reenter woods.

2.2   Reach paved Long House Road (Brady Road). Turn left, and follow road for 375 feet, then turn right, and reenter woods.

2.3   Turn right onto old woods road for 40 feet, then turn left, and cross logs over intermittent stream.

2.5   Ascend steeply under hemlock tree.

2.6   Make sharp left turn.

2.9   Cross old woods road.

3.1   Cross brook.

3.2   Ascend very steeply, with stone wall to right.

3.3   Join old farm road that comes in from left. In another 125 feet, road curves to the left and continues along right side of an overgrown field.

3.4   At end of the field, bear left, and follow road along edge of field, then turn right, and reenter woods.

3.5   Turn left, and cross remains of old stone wall.

3.6   Cross paved Warwick Turnpike.

3.8   Cross plank bridge over swamp outlet, and begin to ascend.

3.9   Turn right, and continue to ascend. In another 200 feet, join woods road coming in from left. (To left, blue-blazed trail leads 0.3 mile to headquarters of Wawayanda State Park.)

4.0 Blue-blazed trail on left leads 0.1 mile up a small rise to **Wawayanda Shelter.**

4.2 Turn left onto dirt Wawayanda Road.

4.4 Turn right onto woods road.

4.6 Reach crest of rise, and begin gradual descent.

4.8 Bear right at fork, and continue along grassy woods road, with long-abandoned, overgrown field on left.

4.9 Turn left on dirt Iron Mountain Road (not passable by car). In another 175 feet, driveway on left leads to stone foundations of the Kazmar house, built about 1815 and demolished in 1991.

5.1 Cross iron bridge over the Doublekill. In another 75 feet, turn right on old woods road.

5.2 Pass overgrown clearing to the left of the Trail.

5.5 Turn left, leaving road. In 100 feet, turn right, and cross stream.

5.7 Make sharp left turn onto old woods road.

6.0 Turn left onto wide woods road, and descend.

6.1 Cross drain, and continue along woods road, with open field to right. This is part of the High Breeze Farm, also known as the Barrett Farm, one of the last intact 19th-century Highland farms in New Jersey. It is now part of Wawayanda State Park and listed in the state and national registers of historic places. The farm is being restored; at present, it is closed to the public.

6.3 Cross small stream, descend stone steps, and turn right onto paved Barrett Road. In 40 feet, turn left, climb wooden steps, and enter field.

6.4 Cross old stone wall, with broken barbed-wire fence, and enter woods, ascending gradually.

6.5 Cross small stream on rocks, and descend slightly, then resume ascent.

6.7 Reach top of ascent, with limited view to right through trees. Trail curves to the left, briefly leveling off, passes Luthers Rock, and begins steady descent.

7.0 Cross small stream. In another 300 feet, cross a stone wall.

7.1 Turn left, and begin to parallel stream.

7.2 Cross a branch stream near a small waterfall.

7.3 Turn left, away from stream, and begin to ascend.

7.4 With house in sight to the left, begin to descend.

7.5 Cross stream on log bridge. In 250 feet, bear right, cross a small tributary stream and then the main stream on a log bridge, and begin to ascend.

7.7 Cross old woods road, and begin short descent. In 150 feet, cross wide stone wall.

7.9 Cross another stone wall, and ascend. In 150 feet, turn left, pass through gap in stone wall, and make short descent.

8.0 Begin gradual ascent.

8.2 Turn right, as blue-blazed Wawayanda Ridge Trail, which continues straight ahead, leads 0.8 mile to viewpoint over Vernon Valley and Pochuck Mountain. In another 50 feet, reach Trail register on tree to left of Trail at crest of Wawayanda Mountain. Please sign register. In 175 feet, begin descent of mountain on stone steps.

8.3 Blue-blazed side trail on the right leads 0.1 mile to Pinwheel's Vista, with spectacular views of Shawangunks and Catskills to the north and Vernon Valley, Pochuck Mountain, and the Kittatinny Ridge to the west and south. In another 250 feet, descend long series of stone steps.

8.4 At base of descent, turn left, and parallel base of cliff on left for 200 feet, then switch back to right, and descend steeply.

8.5 Briefly parallel base of cliff on left.

8.7 Turn right, and proceed west, away from mountain, for 250 feet, then turn right again, and go north, parallel to mountain, continuing to descend.

8.9 Pass Annie's Bluff to the right, then descend two small switchbacks and stone steps, and continue gradual descent.

9.1 Reach base of Wawayanda Mountain. Turn right, continuing along base of mountain for about 500 feet, then turn left, away from mountain.

9.2 Cross old stone wall, and emerge from woods onto field, with views of Vernon Valley and Pochuck Mountain.

9.4 Cross gravel quarry road, and descend slightly down grassy path between stone drains.

9.6 Pass through A.T. parking area, and reach N.J. 94 (end of section). To continue, proceed straight across Route 94 into field.

Trail Description, South to North

Miles   **Data**

0.0 From N.J. 94, proceed east, passing through A.T. parking area, and ascend grassy path between stone drains.

0.2 Cross gravel quarry road, and continue gentle ascent through field.

0.4 Cross old stone wall, and enter woods.

0.5 Reach base of Wawayanda Mountain. Turn right, and continue along base of mountain, then turn left, and begin gradual ascent of Wawayanda escarpment.

0.8 Turn left, climb stone steps, ascend two small switchbacks, and pass Annie's Bluff to the right.

1.0 Turn left, and proceed east, toward mountain, for 250 feet, then turn left again, and go north, parallel to the mountain, continuing to ascend.

1.1 Briefly parallel base of cliff on right.

1.2 After switchback to right and steep ascent, turn left, and parallel cliff on right. In another 200 feet, begin ascent of long series of stone steps.

1.3 Blue-blazed side trail on the left leads 0.1 mile to Pinwheel's Vista, with spectacular views of Shawangunks and Catskills to the north and Vernon Valley, Pochuck Mountain, and the Kittatinny Ridge to the west and south. In another 75 feet, turn right, and ascend more steeply.

1.5 Climb the last set of stone steps to top of Wawayanda Mountain escarpment. In 175 feet, reach and sign Trail register on tree to right of Trail. In another 50 feet, blue-blazed Wawayanda Ridge Trail on right leads 0.8 mile to viewpoint over Vernon Valley and Pochuck Mountain. Turn left, and begin to descend.

1.8 After short ascent, pass through gap in stone wall, then turn right, and descend. In 150 feet, cross another stone wall.

2.0 Cross wide stone wall, and begin short ascent. In 150 feet, cross old woods road, and soon begin descent.

2.1 Cross stream on log bridge, then cross small tributary stream, and bear left. In 250 feet, cross another stream on log bridge, ascend, make sharp left turn, and begin to parallel stream to left.

2.2   With house in sight to right, begin to descend.

2.3   Begin to parallel stream more closely.

2.4   Cross a branch stream near a small waterfall.

2.5   Turn right, away from stream, and begin ascent. In 250 feet, cross a stone wall.

2.9   Reach top of ascent. Trail briefly levels off, passes Luthers Rock, then begins descent, with limited view ahead through trees as Trail curves to the right.

3.1   Trail curves to right and ascends slightly. In another 400 feet, cross small stream on rocks, and continue gradual descent.

3.2   Cross old stone wall, with broken barbed-wire fence, and enter field. In 250 feet, bear right at post.

3.3   Descend wooden steps, and turn right onto paved Barrett Road. Directly to the north is the High Breeze Farm, also known as the Barrett Farm, one of the last intact 19th-century Highland farms in New Jersey. It is now part of Wawayanda State Park and listed in the state and national registers of historic places. The farm is being restored; at present, it is closed to the public. Continue along Barrett Road for 40 feet, turn left, climb stone steps, cross small stream, and continue along woods road, with open field to left.

3.5   At end of field, cross drain, and begin to ascend.

3.6   At crest of hill, turn right onto old woods road.

3.9   Make sharp right turn, leaving road.

4.1   Cross stream, and turn left. In 100 feet, turn right on old woods road.

4.4   Pass overgrown clearing to right of Trail.

4.5   Turn left on dirt Iron Mountain Road (not passable by car), and cross iron bridge over the Doublekill.

4.7   Driveway on right leads to stone foundations of the Kazmar house, built about 1815 and demolished in 1991. In another 175 feet, turn right onto grassy woods road, passing long-abandoned, overgrown field on right.

4.8   Take left fork.

5.0   Reach crest of rise, and begin gradual descent.

5.2   Turn left onto dirt Wawayanda Road.

5.4   Turn right onto woods road.
5.6   Blue-blazed trail on right leads 0.1 mile up a small rise to **Wawayanda Shelter.**
5.7   Bear left at fork in road, and begin to descend. To right, blue-blazed trail leads 0.3 mile to headquarters of Wawayanda State Park. In another 200 feet, turn left, and continue to descend.
5.8   Cross plank bridge over swamp outlet.
6.0   Cross paved Warwick Turnpike.
6.1   Cross remains of old stone wall, and turn right.
6.2   Leave woods, turn left, and follow old farm road along left side of overgrown field.
6.3   Bear right at fork in road. In another 125 feet, continue straight ahead as road curves to right, and reenter woods.
6.4   Descend very steeply, with stone wall to the left.
6.5   Cross brook.
6.7   Cross old woods road.
7.0   Make sharp right turn. In another 350 feet, descend steeply under hemlock tree.
7.3   Cross logs over intermittent stream, turn right onto old woods road for 40 feet, then turn left, and ascend into woods.
7.4   Reach paved Long House Road (Brady Road). Turn left, and follow road for 375 feet, then turn right, and reenter woods.
7.6   Turn right onto grassy woods road.
7.7   Turn left, and reenter woods.
7.9   Turn right onto woods road for 35 feet, then turn left, and reenter woods.
8.1   Cross log bridge over stream.
8.5   Cross split-log bridge over Long House Creek.
8.6   Turn left onto dirt road for 45 feet, then turn right, and ascend into woods.
8.7   Cross woods road. In 450 feet, cross another woods road.
8.9   Cross small stream using rocks.
9.1   Reach rock ledge with view to west.
9.3   At junction with yellow-blazed Ernest Walter Trail, the A.T. turns left and continues along rock ledges. Ernest Walter Trail makes a loop around West Pond and Surprise Lake and connects in about 1.0 mile with the white-blazed

Bearfort Ridge Trail, which leads 2.5 miles south to Warwick Turnpike.

9.4   Reach crest of Bearfort Mountain, with eastern views over Surprise Lake and Sterling Ridge.

9.6   Reach blue-blazed State Line Trail (end of section). To continue, proceed straight ahead (see New York Section Thirteen).

N.J. 94 to N.J. 284 (Unionville, New York)
New Jersey Section Two
11.6 Miles

Brief Description of Section

This section of the Trail passes through Vernon Valley, continues along hard-surfaced roads, and follows woods roads and paths over Pochuck Mountain. It then passes through a sod farm, following the dikes, briefly follows a paved road across the Wallkill River, and continues through woods and farms.

This region exhibits the influence of glaciation, particularly in the mucky soils of Vernon Valley, a former glacial lake. Pochuck Mountain, a block of resistant metamorphic gneiss, represents the high point and drainage divide between Vernon Valley and Kittatinny Valley.

The eastern portion of this section of the Trail was relocated in the 1990s from roads to a Trail corridor acquired by the state of New Jersey. However, the Trail still follows paved roads for about two miles. Be alert to the painted blazes, and, if they deviate from the printed Trail description, follow the blazes in preference to the printed data.

Portions of the Trail in this section still pass through private property. Please be respectful of the rights of the landowners who have generously allowed the Trail to be routed through their property until the completion of the permanent route in the corridor acquired by the state.

Few dependable sources of potable water are available along this section, so plan to bring along sufficient water.

Road Approaches

Both the northern and southern ends of this section are accessible by vehicle. The northern end of the section is on N.J. 94, about 0.6 mile north of the intersection of N.J. 94 and Maple Grange Road and about 2.4 miles north of Vernon. A designated parking area is at the Trail crossing. At the southern end, the Trail crosses N.J. 284,

0.9 mile south of the center of Unionville, New York. Parking for four or five cars is available in a dirt turnout just north of the Trail crossing (overnight parking not encouraged).

Public Transportation

No public transportation is available at either end of this section.

Maps

For route navigation, refer to Map Four of this guide. For area detail, refer to the following USGS 7½-minute topographic quadrangles: Wawayanda, New Jersey-New York; Hamburg, New Jersey; Unionville, New York-New Jersey.

Shelters and Campsites

This section has one shelter:

Pochuck Mountain Shelter: Built in 1988-89 by local volunteers with assistance from the ATC Mid-Atlantic Trail Crew; 7.4 miles from northern end of section; 4.2 miles from southern end of section; 0.1 mile from the A.T. on blue-blazed side trail; accommodates 6; water from hand pump located 0.4 mile to the south, at crossing of Wallkill Road (Liberty Corners Road). (Water tested for potability by N.J. State Park Service.)

Next shelter: north 13.0 miles (Wawayanda Shelter); south 12.4 miles (High Point Shelter).

Supplies and Services

At the northern end of this section, a seasonal farm market is 0.1 mile to the north along N.J. 94, and a shopping center, with a 24-hour supermarket, a pizzeria, a deli, restaurants, and a post office (ZIP Code 07462), is in Vernon, 2.4 miles south of the Trail crossing along N.J. 94 and County 515. At the southern end of the section, groceries, meals, and a post office (ZIP Code 10988) are available in Unionville, New York, on N.Y. 284, 0.9 mile north of the Trail crossing.

Public Accommodations

At the northern end of the section, the Appalachian Motel is 1.4 miles south of the Trail crossing along N.J. 94. The Apple Valley Inn, a historic farmhouse, is one mile north of the Trail crossing of County 565 (hikers are offered discounts on lodging). No accommodations are available at the southern end of the section.

Trail Description, North to South

Miles	Data
0.0	Proceed west from N.J. 94, and cross stepstile into field (cow pasture). Bear left to post and puncheon at center of field, and cross puncheon.
0.2	At field edge, climb over second stepstile. Climb embankment, and cross railroad tracks diagonally to the right. (The railroad was built in 1881 at the Lehigh and Hudson River. It is now part of the New York, Susquehanna and Western Railway.) Descend to stepstile, then cross over stile, and follow puncheon through a second field.
0.3	Enter woods. In another 300 feet, leave woods, and cross over stepstile into old field overgrown with trees. Climb knoll.
0.4	Descend slightly from knoll, cross overgrown fence row, pass through post stile into fourth field, and follow posts across field.
0.7	Make sharp left onto bridge over Wawayanda Creek. Go through post stile, cross farm road, and climb gently uphill, then follow posts across field (cow pasture).
0.9	Cross over stepstile, and turn left onto Canal Road. The large stream on the right is the canal itself, dug in the mid-19th century to divert water from Wawayanda Creek and thus help drain the Vernon meadows.
1.4	Turn right onto paved Maple Grange Road.
1.6	Cross one-lane bridge over Black Creek.
2.2	Turn right onto County 517.
3.0	Turn left, cross stile over stone wall, and cross wet area on puncheon, then ascend slightly over rise.

3.1   Reach top of rise. Cross wet area on puncheon, and descend across open fields, following posts.

3.2   Reach end of field, reenter woods, and begin ascent.

3.5   Reach eastern viewpoint over Wawayanda Mountain, then pass through stand of red cedars, and cross stone wall, continuing to ascend.

3.6   Trail levels off.

3.8   Begin to descend.

3.9   Cross old woods road.

4.0   Trail levels off.

4.2   Trail runs parallel to stone wall on right. Soon begin to ascend, crossing several stone walls.

4.5   Descend from shoulder of hill.

4.6   Cross field, and reach paved County 565. On the left is the former Glenwood School, built in 1864 and used until 1958. Cross road, and follow posts across field.

4.7   Cross wooden bridge over stream, then pass through gap in stone wall. Begin to ascend.

4.8   Pass through old field, now overgrown with red cedars, then bear right, and continue across field.

4.9   At end of field, turn left, and continue along right side of field, with tree line to right.

5.0   Turn right, and reenter woods. In another 150 feet, cross swampy area on puncheon, then cross stream on rocks.

5.2   Cross private dirt road.

5.5   Cross swampy area on puncheon.

5.8   Reach summit of Pochuck Mountain. Side trail to the right leads 40 feet to viewpoint over west ridge of mountain. Begin to descend.

6.0   Cross private dirt road, and continue to descend. In another 250 feet, cross swampy area on puncheon as Trail levels off. Soon pass through hemlock grove.

6.1   Turn right as the former Trail route comes in from the left.

6.2   Join old woods road, which comes in from the right. Follow road for 150 feet, then turn right, leaving road. Begin gradual ascent.

6.5   Reach beautiful overlook, with western views across Wallkill Valley to High Point and the Kittatinnies. Continue along crest of middle ridge of Pochuck Mountain.

6.6   Begin to descend, first gradually, then more steeply.

6.8   Turn left onto woods road for 30 feet, then turn right, and begin to ascend.

7.1   Reach summit of western ridge of Pochuck Mountain, and begin to descend on switchbacks.

7.4   Blue-blazed trail on right leads 0.1 mile to **Pochuck Mountain Shelter.**

7.7   Emerge onto open field. Continue across field, then cross stone wall and row of trees, and emerge onto overgrown field. Follow posts downhill across field.

7.8   Reach paved Wallkill Road (also known as Liberty Corners Road). Turn right, and follow road for 120 feet, then cross road, reenter woods, and reach water pump.

7.9   Follow puncheon for about 0.4 mile across wet area.

8.3   Ascend wooden steps, and turn left onto dirt road (the abandoned right-of-way of the Lehigh and New England Railroad, built in 1888 and abandoned in 1961). Follow dirt road along east side of Liberty Sod Farms.

8.6   Turn right, and follow dike across sod farm.

8.9   Road makes jog to the right, then to the left, and continues along the south side of sod farm.

9.1   Turn right, and continue on road along western side of sod farm.

9.8   Turn left onto paved Oil City Road.

10.1   Cross bridge over Wallkill River.

10.3   Turn left onto paved road leading into Carnegie Industries (private property). Carnegie's large brick building—once a pumping station for the 1880s' Olean-Bayonne oil pipeline of the Standard Oil Company—gave Oil City its name. A huge tank farm once stood nearby.

10.5   Turn right, and reenter woods. In another 75 feet, cross bridge over small stream.

10.6   Cross stone wall.

10.8   Emerge onto open field, and turn left. In another 300 feet, cross row of trees, then turn right, following edge of field uphill, with corn field on left.

11.0   At top of hill, turn left, and follow edge of field. In another 200 feet, turn right, pass through opening in barbed-wire fence, and descend through overgrown field.

11.1   Cross paved Oil City Road (different from the previous road with same name), and enter field, following stone wall to the left. Then, turn right, and follow posts diagonally across field.

11.3   At end of field, descend, and cross through hollow, then bear left, and ascend from hollow.

11.4   At top of ascent, bear left, continue along left edge of field for 200 feet to end of field, bear left again, and descend.

11.6   Follow puncheon through swampy thickets, cross bridge over brook, and reach N.J. 284 (end of section). To continue, cross road, and follow Trail uphill into woods (see New Jersey Section Three).

Trail Description, South to North

Miles   Data

0.0   From N.J. 284, cross bridge over brook, and follow puncheon through swampy thickets. Cross over stone wall, and bear right, climbing small knoll.

0.2   Reach top of knoll. Continue along right side of field for 200 feet, then turn right, and descend. Cross through hollow, and ascend.

0.3   Reach open field. Follow posts diagonally across field, then turn left at stone wall (edge of woods), and follow along edge of field.

0.5   Reach paved Oil City Road. Cross road, and ascend gradually through overgrown field.

0.6   Pass through opening in barbed-wire fence, and turn left, following edge of field uphill, with corn field to right. In 200 feet, reach top of hill, and turn right, following edge of field.

0.8   Turn left, and cross row of trees. In another 300 feet, turn right, and reenter woods.

1.0   Cross stone wall.

1.1   Cross bridge over small stream. In another 75 feet, turn left onto paved road, property of Carnegie Industries. Carnegie's large brick building—once a pumping station for the 1880s' Olean-Bayonne oil pipeline of the Standard Oil Company—gave Oil City its name.

1.3   Turn right onto State Line Road.

1.5   Cross bridge over Wallkill River. Name of road changes to Oil City Road.

1.8   Turn right onto driveway leading into Liberty Sod Farms. Continue straight ahead on dirt road, with sod farm to left.

2.5   Sod-farm road makes left turn. Continue on road along the south side of sod farm.

2.7   Road makes jog to the right, then to left, and continues on dike across sod farm.

3.0   At end of sod farm, turn left, and follow dirt road (abandoned railroad right-of-way) along east side of the sod farm. This was the route of the Lehigh and New England Railroad, built in 1888 and abandoned in 1961.

3.3   Turn right, descend wooden steps, and follow puncheon for about 0.4 mile across wet area.

3.8   Reach water pump (only source of water for Pochuck Mountain Shelter, 0.5 mile ahead on Trail), then reach paved Wallkill Road (also known as Liberty Corners Road). Turn right, follow road for 120 feet, cross road, and follow posts uphill across overgrown field.

3.9   Cross row of trees and stone wall, continue across second field, reenter woods, and begin to ascend on switchbacks.

4.2   Blue-blazed trail on left leads 0.1 mile to **Pochuck Mountain Shelter**.

4.5   Reach summit of western ridge of Pochuck Mountain, and begin to descend.

4.8   Turn left onto woods road for 30 feet, then turn right, and resume ascent. In about 500 feet, begin steeper ascent on rocky trail.

5.0   Reach crest of middle ridge of Pochuck Mountain, and bear right, following ridge.

5.1   Reach beautiful overlook, with western views across Wallkill Valley to High Point and the Kittatinnies. Begin gradual descent.

5.4   Turn left onto old woods road. Follow road for 150 feet, then bear right onto Trail as road turns left.

5.5   Turn left on relocated Trail, as old Trail route continues straight ahead, and pass through hemlock grove.

5.6   Cross swampy area on puncheon, and begin to ascend. In another 250 feet, cross dirt private road, and continue to ascend.

5.8   Reach summit of Pochuck Mountain. Side trail to left leads 40 feet to viewpoint over western ridge of mountain. Begin to descend.

6.1   Cross swampy area on puncheon, and continue descent.

6.4   Cross private dirt road.

6.6   Cross stream on rocks, then cross swampy area on puncheon. In another 150 feet, emerge onto open field. Continue along left side of field, with tree line to right.

6.7   Turn right, and cross field, then bear left, descending through old field now overgrown with red cedars. Continue steady descent.

6.9   Pass through gap in stone wall, climb steps, and cross wooden bridge over stream, then follow posts across field.

7.0   Reach paved County 565. On the right is the former Glenwood School, built in 1864 and used until 1958. Cross road, continue across field, enter woods, and ascend to shoulder of hill.

7.1   Begin to descend, crossing several stone walls.

7.4   Trail runs parallel to stone wall on left, then turns away from stone wall, and ascends briefly.

7.6   Begin steady ascent.

7.7   Cross old woods road, and continue to ascend.

7.8   Trail levels off.

8.0   Bear right, and begin steady descent.

8.1   Cross stone wall, and pass through stand of red cedars. In another 150 feet, reach eastern viewpoint over Wawayanda Mountain. Continue to descend.

8.4   At base of descent, emerge onto open fields. Continue across fields, following posts. Cross wet area on puncheon, and ascend slightly over rise.

8.5   Reach top of rise, and begin to descend.

8.6   Cross wet area on puncheon, cross stile over stone wall, and reach paved County 517. Turn right, and follow road.

9.4   Turn left onto Maple Grange Road.

10.0   Cross one-lane bridge over Black Creek.

10.2   Turn left off Maple Grange Road onto Canal Road.

10.7   Just before reaching Canal Road dead-end at Pochuck Creek, turn right, and cross stepstile into field (cow pasture), with excellent views of Wawayanda Mountain. The large stream on the left is the canal itself, dug in the mid-

19th century to divert water from Wawayanda Creek and thus help drain the Vernon meadows. Follow posts across field, then descend gently.

10.9   Cross farm road, pass through post stile, and cross bridge over Wawayanda Creek. Immediately turn right, and continue along edge of second field, then follow posts across field.

11.1   Go through post stile, and cross third field on puncheon. Pass through overgrown fence row, climb knoll, and descend slightly through old field overgrown with trees.

11.3   Cross old stone wall, cross over stepstile, and enter woods. In another 300 feet, leave woods, and follow puncheon across fourth field.

11.4   At field edge, cross over a stepstile. Climb embankment, and cross railroad tracks diagonally to the right. (The railroad was built in 1881 as the Lehigh and Hudson River. It is now part of the New York, Susquehanna and Western Railway.) Descend to stepstile, climb over stile, and cross cow pasture on puncheon. At end of puncheon in midpasture, bear left toward another stepstile.

11.6   Cross stepstile, and reach N.J. 94 (end of section). To continue, proceed straight across N.J. 94.

N.J. 284 (Unionville, New York) to N.J. 23 (High Point, New Jersey)
New Jersey Section Three
9.9 Miles

Brief Description of Section

This section of the Trail completes the crossing of the Kittatinny Valley traveling south along the Trail. It continues to parallel the New York-New Jersey state line while heading in a northwesterly direction. From N.J. 284, the Trail passes through rolling farmlands, pastures, fields, and open woods before climbing to the eastern face of the Kittatinny Ridge. It is pleasant and easy walking. The southern portion of this section is in High Point State Park and passes just below High Point Monument, which marks the highest elevation in New Jersey (1,803 feet). Completed in 1930, High Point Monument was built through the generosity of Colonel Anthony R. Kuser and his wife, Susie Dryden Kuser, and is dedicated to "New Jersey's heroes by land, sea, and air in all wars in our country." Colonel and Mrs. Kuser also donated the original 10,500 acres of High Point State Park to the people of New Jersey in 1923. A blue-blazed side trail (0.3 mile round-trip) leads to the monument, but much the same panorama of New Jersey, Pennsylvania, and New York is provided from a wooden observation platform directly on the Trail. The Trail turns southwesterly along the ridge to the southern terminus of the section at High Point State Park headquarters.

This section was the first portion of the A.T. in New Jersey to be relocated within the protected Appalachian Trail corridor acquired by the state of New Jersey. It was opened on October 2, 1982, in a ceremony attended by the governor, at which time a cooperative agreement between the NY-NJTC and the state for the maintenance of the Trail was signed.

Road Approaches

Both the northern and southern ends of this section are accessible by vehicle. At the northern end, the Trail crosses N.J. 284, 0.9 mile south of the center of Unionville, New York. Parking for four or five cars is available in a dirt turnout just north of the Trail crossing (overnight parking not encouraged). At the southern end, the Trail crosses N.J. 23 at the southern driveway of High Point State Park headquarters. A parking lot specifically for A.T. hikers is located just south of park headquarters (registration required for overnight parking). Parking for day hikes is also available at the Trail crossing of County 519. The Trail in this section also crosses numerous secondary roads and lanes, but parking along these roads is not recommended.

Public Transportation

Bus service to New York City, operated by Short Line Bus System, (201) 529-3666, is available at Port Jervis, New York, about seven miles northwest of the Trail crossing of N.J. 23 (follow N.J. 23 north to junction with U.S. 6; continue west on U.S. 6). Rail service to New York City (via Hoboken), operated by the Metro-North Commuter Railroad, (212) 532-4900 or (800) 638-7646, is also available. Public transportation is not available at the northern end of the section.

Maps

For route navigation, refer to Maps Four and Five with this guide. For area detail, refer to the following USGS 7½-minute topographic quadrangles: Unionville, New York-New Jersey; Port Jervis South, New Jersey-New York-Pennsylvania.

Shelters and Campsites

This section has one shelter:
High Point Shelter: Built in 1936 by the Civilian Conservation Corps; stone shelter with wooden floor; 8.2 miles from northern end of section; 1.7 miles from southern end of section; 0.1 mile from

A.T. on blue-blazed side trail; accommodates 8; water available from streams near shelter.

Next shelter: north 12.4 miles (Pochuck Mountain Shelter); south 4.2 miles (Rutherford Shelter).

Supplies and Services

At the northern end of the section, groceries, sandwiches, and a post office (ZIP Code 10988) are available in Unionville, New York, on N.Y. 284, 0.9 mile north of the Trail crossing. Unionville also may be reached via Lott Road (also known as Jersey Avenue), which crosses the Trail one mile from the northern end of the section (follow Lott Road to the north for 0.3 mile, then turn left along N.Y. 284 for 0.1 mile).

The southern end has supermarkets and a laundromat on N.J. 23, 4.3 miles northwest of the Trail crossing. Groceries are also available in Colesville, 2.5 miles southeast of the Trail crossing on N.J. 23. Supermarkets, restaurants, and a post office (ZIP Code 12771) are located in Port Jervis, New York, about seven miles northwest of the Trail crossing of N.J. 23 (follow N.J. 23 north to junction with U.S. 6; continue west on U.S. 6). During the summer season, refreshments are available at a concession stand near the High Point Monument. The headquarters of High Point State Park, at the southern end of the section, will accept and hold packages for hikers if marked "hold for arrival" with the name of the hiker and the approximate date of arrival specified (address: High Point State Park, Sussex, NJ 07461).

Public Accommodations

At the southern end of the section, motels are located on N.J. 23 1.4 miles south and 4.4 miles north of the Trail crossing. No accommodations are available at the northern end of the section.

Trail Description, North to South

Miles   Data

0.0   From N.J. 284, enter woods, and ascend for 250 feet to field. Turn right, and skirt field, keeping tree line on right, and turn left up slope of field.

0.3   At end of the field, ascend to abandoned railroad grade. Turn right, and follow railroad grade.

0.8   Bear left, leaving railroad grade, and follow stone wall paralleling railroad grade below. After 350 feet, turn left, and continue into woods, crossing two stone walls.

1.0   Pass pond to right of the Trail, and reach paved Lott Road (also known as Jersey Avenue. Unionville, New York, is 0.4 mile to the right along Lott Road, then left on N.Y. 284). Turn right, cross bridge over stream, and continue along road for 175 feet, then turn left, and ascend into woods, passing house to right of Trail.

1.1   Enter open field, and bear right across field.

1.2   Reenter woods, and ascend gradually, crossing numerous old quarry roads. This area was famous in the 19th century for its production of bluestone, widely used as a paving material.

1.5   Reach crest of hill, and begin to descend, following left fork of trail.

1.7   Reach paved Quarry Road. Cross road, and reenter woods, passing old quarry pit and house on right.

2.0   Reach paved Unionville Road (County 651). Cross road diagonally to left, and reenter woods.

2.1   Cross stone wall, and emerge onto open field. Continue straight ahead, ascending hill. Cross farm road, and continue ahead on another old farm road. In 150 feet, turn left, and pass through field break. Continue through another field break, then pass through abandoned apple orchard.

2.4   Reach dirt Goldsmith Lane. Cross road, and enter overgrown successional field. In 300 feet, bear right, and cross stone wall.

2.5   Follow puncheon across Vernie Swamp for next 0.3 mile.

2.8   Cross bridge over stream. In another 100 feet, cross gravel Goldsmith Road, then climb through field, keeping trees and low stone wall (New York-New Jersey boundary) to right.

3.0   Reach crest of field, with excellent view of High Point Monument directly ahead. To rear, Pochuck Mountain is on the horizon. Descend, with pines on right.

3.1   Pass pond to left, crossing concrete dam (outlet of pond). Emerge onto field. Cross field, bearing left, and reenter woods. Continue over gentle hill.

3.2   Reach crest of hill, and descend.

3.3   Reach paved Goodrich Road. Cross road, pass briefly through woods, and enter overgrown field.

3.4   Cross small stream.

3.6   Bear left, then turn right, and cross log bridge over stream. In another 200 feet, cross bridge over second stream, turn left, and ascend.

3.9   Reach crest of rise, and begin to descend.

4.0   Pass through very muddy area. Cross stream, and bear right.

4.1   Follow stone wall to the left for 200 feet. Reach intersection of stone walls, with fence on right wall. Turn right, and, in 60 feet, come out on successional field with cedars. Continue through field, bearing right.

4.2   Turn right, and cross brook, then follow posts across overgrown field.

4.3   Reach paved Gemmer Road. Turn right, and follow road for 200 feet, then turn left, and reenter woods, passing through swampy area.

4.4   Turn left, and cross small brook. Bear right, and ascend, passing through swampy area.

4.5   Emerge onto abandoned field, and follow posts diagonally to left across field.

4.6   Cross stone wall, and reenter woods.

4.9   Reach Ferguson Road (passable by car). Turn right, and follow road for 120 feet, then turn left, cross stile, and enter pasture. Follow blazes across pasture.

5.0   Cross boggy area on puncheon, then cross bridge over stream. Bear left, and follow posts across pasture, crossing muddy area.

5.1   At intersection of stone walls, bear right, and cross over stile into cultivated field. (This section of Trail corridor is being farmed under lease arrangement with former owner, whose family has worked the land for five generations.) Skirt field, following tree line on left.

5.2   At end of field, turn right, continuing to follow tree line on left, then cross overgrown stone wall, and turn left. Again skirt field, following tree line on left.

5.4   At end of field, turn right, continuing to follow tree line on left, then turn left, passing pond on right. Cross over stile, and turn right, skirting field. In another 300 feet, turn right, and pass through electrified gate at farm maintenance road. *Use care, and close gate.* Turn left, and ascend along left side of pasture.

5.6   Cross barbed-wire fence near crest of pasture, and descend along left side of cultivated fields.

5.7   Pass through stile, and reenter woods.

5.9   Follow blazes carefully across and along many old stone walls.

6.1   Reach dirt-and-gravel Courtwright Road (passable by car). Cross road, and continue straight ahead through woods.

6.2   Cross stream.

6.3   Cross grassy woods road, cross stream, and emerge onto overgrown field. Continue across field.

6.4   Reenter woods, and cross swampy area, then cross several stone walls.

6.8   Leave woods, and pass through fields, skirting to right of trees on rise.

6.9   Reach paved County 519. Cross road, bearing slightly to left, and reenter woods, ascending on switchbacks.

7.1   After passing through swampy area, emerge onto overgrown clearing. In 175 feet, turn left onto dirt road, and follow road for 150 feet, then turn right, and pass through pasture.

7.2   Turn right, and ascend, with views to right, then make sharp left turn, and continue to ascend.

7.4   Trail bears left and levels off, passing through gaps in several stone walls.

8.0   Cross intermittent brook at head of ravine, bear left, and pass over stone wall. In another 150 feet, the Trail turns right at intersection. Former Trail route descends along ravine. *Do not descend.*

8.2   Turn right, and ascend. Blue-blazed side trail continues straight ahead 0.1 mile to **High Point Shelter.** Water is available from streams before and beyond shelter.

8.7   Turn left at intersection with blue-blazed side trail, which leads north to High Point Monument, marking the highest elevation in New Jersey (1,803 feet).

8.9   Reach wooden observation platform. Excellent 360-degree view. Kittatinny Valley lies to the east, with Pochuck Mountain in the distance and Wawayanda Mountain on the horizon. New York City skyline may be visible to the southeast. To the southwest is Delaware Water Gap. In foreground to the west are Lake Marcia and High Point Lodge, with the Pocono Mountains of Pennsylvania in the distance. Catskill Plateau lies northwest. High Point Monument dominates the ridge to the north. Continue south along ridge, passing through scrub oak and blueberry bushes.

9.0   Bear right, and continue along ridge, as former Trail route descends from ridge.

9.1   Turn left, and descend, as former Trail route continues straight ahead. In another 200 feet, descend steeply, then continue descending more moderately.

9.8   Leave woods, and cross lawn.

9.9   Reach paved N.J. 23 (end of section). To continue, cross road at south driveway of High Point State Park headquarters, and reenter woods at south end of parking lot (see New Jersey Section Four). Water is available at headquarters. Please sign Trail register at office desk.

Trail Description, South to North

Miles   Data

0.0   From N.J. 23, bear northeast across lawn for 300 feet, and enter woods. Gradually ascend through scrub oak and blueberry bushes while bearing left, and reach shoulder of ridge.

0.8   Ascend steeply for 180 feet. In another 200 feet, former Trail route enters from left. High Point Monument is visible directly ahead. Trail turns right.

0.9   Bear left, and continue along ridge as former Trail route descends from ridge.

1.0   Reach wooden observation platform. Excellent 360-degree view. Kittatinny Valley, through which Trail passes, lies to the east, with Pochuck Mountain in distance and Wawayanda Mountain on the horizon. New York City skyline may be visible to southeast. To the southwest is Delaware Water Gap. In foreground to the west are Lake Marcia and High Point Lodge, with Pocono Mountains of Pennsylvania in the distance. To the northwest lies Catskill Plateau. Continue along ridge, and descend into saddle below monument.

1.2   Trail turns right and begins descent off ridge. Blue-blazed side trail continues along ridge to High Point Monument, which marks highest elevation in New Jersey (1,803 feet).

1.7   Blue-blazed side trail leads to the right 0.1 mile to **High Point Shelter**. Water is available from streams before and beyond shelter. A.T. turns left.

1.9   Turn left. Abandoned Trail route enters from right. Pass over stone wall, cross intermittent brook at head of ravine, and continue along ridge, passing through gaps in several stone walls.

2.5   Trail bears right, descending off ridge.

2.6   Make sharp right, and continue to descend, with views to left.

2.7   Turn left, and leave woods. Pass through field, and, in 240 feet, turn left on dirt road. Follow dirt road for 150 feet, then turn right. Pass through overgrown clearing, and reenter woods, passing through swampy area.

3.0   Descend on switchbacks, and reach paved County 519. Cross road, bearing slightly to left, and pass through fields, skirting to left of trees on rise.

3.1   Reenter woods, and cross several stone walls.

3.5   Cross swampy area, and emerge onto overgrown field. Continue across field.

3.6   Reenter woods, and cross stream, then cross grassy woods road. In another 350 feet, cross second stream.

3.8   Reach dirt-and-gravel Courtwright Road (passable by car). Cross road, and follow blazes carefully along and through many old stone walls.

4.2   Pass through stile, and enter cultivated fields. Skirt fields to right, following stone wall.

4.3   Cross barbed-wire fence near crest of field, and descend along right side of pasture.

4.4   Near end of field, turn right, and pass through electrified wire gate at farm maintenance road. *Use care, and close gate.* (This section of Trail corridor is being farmed under lease arrangement with former owner.) Skirt left side of field for 300 feet, then turn left, and pass through stile. Pass pond on left.

4.5   At end of pond, bear right, and skirt edge of field. Turn left, and continue along right side of field.

4.6   Turn right, crossing overgrown stone wall, and enter lower field. Again skirt field by keeping tree line on right.

4.8   At intersection of stone walls, cross stile into lower pasture. Bear left, and follow posts across pasture, crossing muddy area. Cross bridge over stream, and walk on puncheon through boggy area. Continue across pasture to road.

5.0   Cross stile, and reach Ferguson Road, passable by car. Turn right, and follow road for 120 feet, then turn left, and reenter woods.

5.3   Cross stone wall, and emerge onto abandoned field. Continue diagonally to the right, following posts through field. Reenter woods, descending gradually, and pass through swampy area.

5.5   Cross small brook, and turn right, passing through swampy area.

5.6   Reach paved Gemmer Road. Turn right, and follow road for 200 feet, then turn left into overgrown field, and follow posts across field.

5.7   Cross brook, and turn left. Continue through successional field with cedars, bearing right.

5.8   Reenter woods. In another 60 feet, reach intersection of stone walls, with fence on right wall. Turn left, and continue with wall on right for 200 feet, then bear left, turning away from wall.

5.9   Cross stream, and bear right, passing through very muddy area.

6.0   Reach crest of rise, and descend gradually, with stream below on right.

6.3   Cross log bridge over stream, and turn left. In another 200 feet, cross bridge over second stream, and bear left. Pass through overgrown field.

6.5   Cross small stream. In another 300 feet, reenter woods.

6.6   Reach paved Goodrich Road. Cross road, and continue up small hill.

6.7   Reach crest of hill, and descend. In 225 feet, cross field.

6.8   With pond on right, reenter woods. In 125 feet, cross concrete dam (outlet of pond). Bear right through pines, then ascend hill, keeping pines on left.

6.9   Reach crest of field, with good view of Pochuck Mountain in the distance. To rear (west) is excellent view of High Point Monument. Trail descends, with trees and low stone wall (New York-New Jersey boundary) on left.

7.1   Cross gravel Goldsmith Road. In another 100 feet, cross bridge over stream, then follow puncheon across Vernie Swamp for next 0.3 mile.

7.4   Cross stone wall, and ascend gradually through overgrown successional field.

7.5   Reach dirt Goldsmith Lane. Cross road, and pass through overgrown apple orchard. Cross overgrown fields, passing through several field breaks.

7.7   Turn right onto old farm road. In 150 feet, reach intersecting farm road. Continue straight ahead down hill, then cross stone wall, and reenter woods.

7.9   Reach paved Unionville Road (County 651). Unionville, N.Y., is 1.2 miles to left. Cross road diagonally to left, and reenter woods, passing house on left and open quarry pit below. This area was famous in the 19th century for its production of bluestone, widely used as a paving material.

8.2   Reach paved Quarry Road. Cross road, and ascend hill.

8.4   Reach crest of hill, and begin to descend. Follow Trail carefully, crossing numerous old quarry roads.

8.7   Emerge onto open field. Follow Trail across field.

8.8   Turn left, and reenter woods. In 125 feet, pass house on left as Trail bears left.

8.9   Reach paved Lott Road (also known as Jersey Avenue. Unionville, N.Y., is 0.4 mile to left along Lott Road, then left again at N.Y. 284). Turn right, and follow road for 175 feet, crossing bridge over stream, then turn left at end of bridge, and reenter woods. Follow shore of pond for 100 feet, then turn right, and continue into woods.

9.1   Turn right, follow old stone wall on left for 350 feet, turn left, and descend to abandoned railroad grade. Turn right, and follow railroad grade.

9.6   Turn left, leaving railroad grade, and descend to field. Skirt field, following tree line to left.

9.9   Turn left, reentering woods, and descend to paved N.J. 284 (end of section). To continue, cross road, and follow Trail straight ahead (see New Jersey Section Two).

N.J. 23 (High Point) to U.S. 206 (Culvers Gap)
New Jersey Section Four
14.3 Miles

Brief Description of Section

The Trail in this section runs along the ridge of the through High Point State Park and Stokes State Forest. The Trail follows a rocky footpath through hickory and scrub-oak forests, with some hemlocks and pitch pines. There are many good viewpoints on both sides of the ridge. The elevation at N.J. 23 is about 1,500 feet; at U.S. 206, it is 935 feet. The highest point in this section is 1,653 feet at Sunrise Mountain.

Many side trails intersect the A.T. in this section. Descriptions of these trails may be found in brochures available at the headquarters of High Point State Park and Stokes State Forest. (Office of High Point is at the northern end of the section; office of Stokes is about 0.5 mile northwest of the southern end of the section along U.S. 206.) These trails are also shown on Maps 17 and 18 of the Kittatinny Trails map set published by the New York-New Jersey Trail Conference.

Road Approaches

Both the northern and southern ends of this section are accessible by vehicle. At the northern end, the Trail crosses N.J. 23 at the southern driveway of High Point State Park headquarters. A parking lot specifically for A.T. hikers is located just south of park headquarters (registration required for overnight parking). At the southern end, the Trail crosses U.S. 206 in Culvers Gap, 3.4 miles northwest of Branchville. A parking area is adjacent to the A.T., 0.3 mile north of the Trail crossing of U.S. 206, on Sunrise Mountain Road, just north of its intersection with Upper North Shore Road (registration at park office required for overnight parking).

Road access is also available at Deckertown Turnpike, which crosses the Trail 5.2 miles from the northern end of the section. In addition, road access is available via Sunrise Mountain Road, which leads to a parking area on Sunrise Mountain, 5.5 miles (along the A.T.) from the southern end of the section. (From U.S. 206, proceed north on Upper North Shore Road for 0.3 mile, turn left on Sunrise Mountain Road, and continue for 4.8 miles to parking area at end of road.)

Public Transportation

Bus service to New York City, operated by Short Line Bus System, (212) 529-3666, is available at Port Jervis, New York, about seven miles northwest of the Trail crossing of N.J. 23 (follow N.J. 23 north to junction with U.S. 6; continue west on U.S. 6). Rail service to New York City (via Hoboken), operated by the Metro-North Commuter Railroad, (212) 532-4900 or (800) 638-7646, is also available. No public transportation is available at the southern end of the section.

Maps

For route navigation, refer to Map Five with this guide. For area detail, refer to the following USGS 7½-minute topographic quadrangles: Port Jervis South, New Jersey-New York-Pennsylvania; Branchville, New Jersey; Culvers Gap, New Jersey-Pennsylvania. Other references are NY-NJ TC Trail Maps 17 and 18 (Kittatinny Trails-North).

Shelters and Campsites

This section has three shelters:

Rutherford Shelter: Built in 1967 by the state of New Jersey; log shelter with wooden floor; 2.5 miles from northern end of section; 11.8 miles from southern end of section; 0.4 mile from A.T. on blue-blazed side trail; accommodates 6; water from nearby spring.

Next shelter: north 4.2 miles (High Point Shelter); south 3.0 miles.

Mashipacong Shelter: Built in 1936; stone shelter with wooden floor; 5.5 miles from northern end of section; 8.8 miles from southern end of section; accommodates 8; water from pump at Trail crossing of Deckertown Turnpike, 0.2 mile to the north along Trail.

Next shelter: north 3.0 miles; south 5.7 miles.

Gren Anderson Shelter: Built in 1958 by New York Section of Green Mountain Club, of which Anderson was a member; log shelter with wooden floor; 11.2 miles from northern end of section; 3.1 miles from southern end of section; 0.3 mile from A.T. on blue-blazed side trail; accommodates 8; water from spring on side trail 200 feet beyond shelter.

Next shelter: north 5.7 miles; south 6.8 miles (Brink Road Shelter).

Supplies and Services

The northern end of the section has supermarkets and a laundromat on N.J. 23, 4.3 miles northwest of the Trail crossing. Groceries are also available in Colesville, 2.5 miles southeast of the Trail crossing on N.J. 23. Supermarkets, restaurants, and a post office (ZIP Code 12771) are located in Port Jervis, New York, about seven miles northwest of the Trail crossing of N.J. 23 (follow N.J. 23 north to junction with U.S. 6; continue west on U.S. 6). The headquarters of High Point State Park, at the northern end of the section, will accept and hold packages for hikers if marked "hold for arrival," with the name of the hiker and the approximate date of arrival specified (address: High Point State Park, Sussex, NJ 07461).

At the southern end of the section, a limited selection of groceries may be obtained at Worthington's Bakery, immediately to the west of the Trail crossing of U.S. 206. A grocery store is located on U.S. 206, 1.6 miles southeast of the Trail crossing. Meals are available at a restaurant 0.1 mile west of the Trail crossing. The Stokes Forest Sport Shop, which sells freeze-dried foods and some camping equipment, is 0.2 mile west. Branchville has a post office (ZIP Code 07826) and a laundromat, 3.4 miles southeast of the Trail crossing of U.S. 206.

Public Accommodations

At the northern end of the section, motels are located on N.J. 23, 1.4 miles south and 4.4 miles north of the Trail crossing. At the southern end, motels are located on U.S. 206, 2.5 miles east and 1.9 miles west of the Trail crossing.

Trail Description, North to South

Miles   **Data**

0.0   From N.J. 23, turn into exit of driveway of parking lot at headquarters of High Point State Park. Please sign register at park headquarters. Reenter woods at south end of parking lot. The yellow-blazed Mashipacong Trail soon joins and runs concurrently with A.T. In 250 feet, pass unmarked trail to left leading to A.T. hikers' parking area.

0.2   Cross old road. Yellow-blazed Mashipacong Trail leaves to right, while red-blazed Iris Trail, marked by white post to left of A.T., follows the old road to the left. (The Iris Trail crosses the A.T. at mileposts 3.3 and 4.6 and can be used to make a circular hike.) Ascend slightly.

0.3   Turn left onto old woods road.

0.4   Turn right, and ascend to ridge.

0.6   Reach crest of ridge, and soon turn left.

0.9   To right, Blue Dot Trail descends to Sawmill Lake.

1.0   Reach viewpoint to west over Sawmill Lake. Descend to left into interior valley.

1.3   Reach valley floor, and ascend steeply to eastern ridge.

1.4   Reach top of eastern ridge at viewpoint back over the valley. Pocono Mountains are visible in the distance to left. Trail crosses to opposite side of ridge.

1.5   Reach limited viewpoint to east from open rocks. Trail continues along ridge.

2.3   Reach beautiful viewpoint from open rocks. To left, Lake Rutherford, water supply for the town of Sussex, is visible. Trail continues along ridge, passing several more viewpoints.

2.5   Reach Dutch Shoe Rock, with views to the northeast. Blue-blazed trail to left descends 0.4 mile to **Rutherford Shelter** and nearby spring. Soon cross large open rocks, then reenter woods, and begin descent.

3.0   Cross stream, and ascend.

3.3   Turn right onto red-blazed Iris Trail (woods road). (To left, Iris Trail can be used as alternate route back to N.J. 23.) In

	300 feet, turn sharp left, leaving Iris Trail, and descend steeply into swampy area.
3.5	Ascend slightly, then descend into another swampy area.
3.7	Cross stream on logs, and ascend gradually.
3.8	Turn left, ascend steeply over rocks, turn right, and continue gradual ascent.
4.2	Cross cleared strip of land (buried pipeline). Short trail to left leads to viewpoint to east over farm landscape. In 140 feet, Trail turns right, away from old road (which continues onto private land).
4.3	Turn right, leaving old Trail route.
4.5	Please sign Trail register on tree to right of Trail.
4.6	Cross red-blazed Iris Trail again. (To right, this trail can be used as an alternate route back to N.J. 23.) A.T. begins to descend.
4.7	Cross rocks over swampy area.
5.0	Pass through swampy area, then ascend gradually.
5.3	Reach parking area and water pump, cross Deckertown Turnpike diagonally to the left, and continue to ascend.
5.5	Reach **Mashipacong Shelter**. Trail reenters woods at far right edge of clearing.
6.2	Turn left onto old woods road (Swenson Road). Follow road for 225 feet, turn right as road curves to left, and ascend on footpath.
6.7	Reach top of rise, and begin to descend, passing through mountain-laurel thicket.
7.0	At base of descent, turn right.
7.1	Cross outlet of swamp to left of Trail. In 250 feet, cross stone wall, and begin to ascend rather steeply through white birches.
7.3	Reach top of hill, and begin to descend.
7.4	Cross stone wall, and continue descent.
7.6	Reach rocky area, and begin to ascend.
7.8	Reach top of knoll, and begin to descend.
8.0	Cross dirt Crigger Road, and ascend.
8.7	Pass parking area for Sunrise Mountain to right of Trail. Restrooms are located here. In 300 feet, path from parking area joins A.T., which continues ascent on wide footpath.
8.9	Reach shelter at summit of Sunrise Mountain (1,653 feet), with good views east and west. The shelter, which was

constructed in the 1930s by the CCC, has a roof but no walls and provides protection from rain, except in high winds. No camping permitted at shelter. From southeast corner of shelter, descend for 150 feet, then come out on open ledges, with beautiful views to east. At southeast corner of clearing, reenter woods, and descend, turning right along rocks.

9.0   Pass viewpoint through trees to left, as Trail briefly levels off then continues gradual descent.

9.4   Ascend over knoll, then descend gradually.

9.8   Reach yellow-blazed Tinsley Trail, which descends to right, crossing Sunrise Mountain Road in 60 yards and continuing to Skellinger Road, about 0.5 mile from Lake Ocquittunk. A.T. ascends briefly and continues along west edge of ridge, with views to west through trees.

10.4   Ascend, then descend gradually.

10.8   For next 0.1 mile, pass several ponds or swamps (in wet season) to left of Trail.

11.1   Pass through several short, wet sections.

11.2   Reach blue-blazed Stony Brook Trail, which leads to right, reaching **Gren Anderson Shelter** in 0.3 mile and spring 200 feet beyond shelter.

11.4   Cross Stony Brook.

12.2   At viewpoint to west in pines, reach green-blazed Tower Trail, which descends to right. Please sign Trail register.

12.3   After brief ascent, reach Culver Fire Tower, which provides 360-degree view. (The tower was erected by the CCC in 1934, replacing an earlier tower.) Lake Owassa is visible to southwest, just left of Kittatinny Ridge, and Lake Kittatinny is visible to right of ridge. Culver Lake is hidden behind the ridge. A.T. continues on footpath at southwest corner of clearing. (To left, gravel road leads to new radio tower.)

12.4   Trail turns right and begins to descend, with Culver Lake soon visible through trees to left.

12.8   Cross small grassy clearing.

13.3   Reach viewpoint over Culver Lake, with view somewhat obscured by trees.

13.4   Turn sharp right. In 200 feet, reach viewpoint to west over Kittatinny Lake. Trail again turns right and continues to descend.

13.5   Turn sharp left, and continue to descend.

13.8   Reach paved Sunrise Mountain Road. Turn left, and follow road for 100 feet, then turn right, and reenter woods.

14.0   Unmarked trail to left leads to A.T. hikers' parking area.

14.3   Reach intersection of Upper North Shore Road (County 636) and U.S. 206 (end of section). To continue, cross Upper North Shore Road, and follow U.S. 206 for 100 feet, then cross U.S. 206 (see New Jersey Section Five).

Trail Description, South to North

Miles   **Data**

0.0   From intersection of U.S. 206 and Upper North Shore Road (County 636), follow Trail northwest into woods.

0.3   Unmarked trail to right leads to A.T. hikers' parking area.

0.5   Reach paved Sunrise Mountain Road. Turn left, and follow road for 100 feet, then turn right, and enter woods, ascending gradually.

0.8   Turn right, and ascend more steeply.

0.9   Turn left at viewpoint over Kittatinny Lake. In 200 feet, turn left again, and continue to ascend, with views of Culver Lake through the trees on the right.

1.0   Reach viewpoint over Culver Lake, with view somewhat obscured by trees.

1.5   Cross small, grassy clearing.

1.9   With radio tower visible ahead, turn left.

2.0   Emerge onto clearing, and reach Culver Fire Tower, which provides 360-degree view. (The tower was erected by the CCC in 1934, replacing an earlier tower.) Lake Owassa is visible to southwest, just left of Kittatinny Ridge, and Lake Kittatinny is visible to right of ridge. Culver Lake is hidden behind ridge. A.T. continues at northwest corner of clearing by a rocky ledge, where it turns right and begins to descend.

2.1   At viewpoint to west in pines, reach green-blazed Tower Trail, which descends to left. Please sign Trail register.

2.3   Bear left at fork in Trail.

2.9   Cross Stony Brook.

3.1   Reach blue-blazed Stony Brook Trail, which leads to left, reaching **Gren Anderson Shelter** in 0.3 mile and spring 200 feet beyond shelter.

3.2   Bear left at fork in Trail, and pass through several short, wet sections.

3.4   For next 0.1 mile, pass several ponds or swamps (in wet season) on right side of Trail.

3.8   Ascend gradually, then descend, coming out on west side of ridge, with views to west through trees.

4.5   After short, steep descent, reach yellow-blazed Tinsley Trail, which descends to left, crossing Sunrise Mountain Road in 60 yards and continuing to Skellinger Road, about 0.5 mile from Lake Ocquittunk.

4.6   Ascend over knoll, then descend.

5.0   Begin gradual ascent of Sunrise Mountain.

5.3   Reach viewpoint through trees to right as Trail levels off.

5.4   After short climb, come out on open ledges, with beautiful views to east. Continue climbing for 150 feet, and reach stone shelter at summit of Sunrise Mountain (1,653 feet), with good views east and west. The shelter, which was constructed in the 1930s by the CCC, has a roof but no walls and provides protection from rain, except in high winds. No camping permitted at shelter. Trail continues on wide footpath from northeast corner of shelter.

5.6   Descend stone steps, then take right fork as wide footpath to left continues to parking area and restrooms. A.T. begins to descend.

6.3   Cross dirt Crigger Road. After short descent, begin to ascend.

6.5   Reach top of knoll, and begin to descend.

6.7   Reach rocky area, and begin to ascend.

6.9   Cross stone wall, and continue to ascend.

7.0   Reach top of hill, and descend steeply through white birches.

7.1   At base of descent, cross stone wall. In 250 feet, cross outlet of swamp to right of Trail.

7.3 Turn left, and begin to ascend, and soon pass through mountain-laurel thicket.

7.6 Reach top of rise, and begin gradual descent.

8.1 Turn left onto old woods road (Swenson Road). Follow road for 225 feet, then turn right, and reenter woods on footpath.

8.8 Reach **Mashipacong Shelter**. Turn left, and descend steadily.

9.0 Cross paved Deckertown Turnpike diagonally to the left, and reach parking area and water pump. Continue to descend.

9.3 Pass through swampy area, and soon begin to ascend.

9.6 Cross rocks over swampy area.

9.7 Cross red-blazed Iris Trail. A.T. levels off and continues along ridge, with limited views through trees to right.

9.8 Please sign Trail register on tree to left of Trail.

10.0 Turn left onto old Trail route.

10.1 Turn left onto woods road. In 140 feet, cross cleared strip of land (buried pipeline). Short trail to right leads to viewpoint to east over farm landscape. Continue along ridge.

10.4 Begin gradual descent.

10.5 Make sharp left turn, and descend steeply over rocks, then turn right, and continue gradual descent.

10.6 Cross stream on logs, and begin gradual ascent.

10.7 Pass small swampy area to left of Trail.

10.8 Make short descent, then continue to ascend.

10.9 After passing through swampy area, begin steep ascent.

11.0 At top of steep ascent, turn right onto red-blazed Iris Trail (woods road). In another 300 feet, turn left, leaving Iris Trail, and ascend briefly, then turn right, and continue along ridge.

11.2 Turn left, and begin to descend.

11.3 Cross stream.

11.5 Begin steady ascent.

11.8 After crossing large open rocks, reach Dutch Shoe Rock, with views to the northeast of Lake Rutherford, the water supply for the town of Sussex. Blue-blazed trail to right descends 0.4 mile to **Rutherford Shelter** and nearby spring. A.T. continues along ridge.

12.0   Reach beautiful viewpoint from open rocks. Trail continues along ridge.

12.8   Reach limited viewpoint from open rocks. Trail turns left and crosses to opposite side of ridge.

12.9   Reach viewpoint to left over interior valley, with Pocono Mountains visible in the distance to the left. Turn left, and descend steeply into the valley.

13.0   Reach floor of valley, and begin ascent to western ridge.

13.3   Reach viewpoint to west over Sawmill Lake. Turn right, and follow ridge.

13.4   To left, Blue Dot Trail descends to Sawmill Lake.

13.7   Turn right, away from ridge, and soon descend steeply.

13.9   Turn left onto old woods road.

14.0   Turn right, leaving road, and descend slightly.

14.1   Cross old road. Yellow-blazed Mashipacong Trail comes in from the left and runs concurrently with the A.T. for 0.2 mile, while red-blazed Iris Trail follows the old road to the right.

14.3   Pass unmarked trail to right leading to A.T. hikers' parking area. In 250 feet, turn right, follow exit driveway of headquarters of High Point State Park (please sign Trail register at park headquarters), and reach N.J. 23 (end of section). To continue, cross N.J. 23 and follow posts across lawn, then enter woods (see New Jersey Section Three).

U.S. 206 (Culvers Gap) to Millbrook-Blairstown Road
New Jersey Section Five
14.6 Miles

Brief Description of Section

This section follows the ridge of the Kittatinny Mountains. The route is mostly wooded, with many good views on both sides of the crest. Although rocky in many areas, the Trail is relatively level, especially in the southern part, with some moderate up-and-down stretches and occasional short, steep sections. The elevation at Millbrook-Blairstown Road, the southern point of the section, is 1,260 feet. The high point of the section—on the ridge north of Crater Lake—is 1,606 feet, and the lowest point is 935 feet, at U.S. 206 in Culvers Gap.

The section passes through oak and hickory hardwood forests, with some conifers, such as pitch pine, white pine, red cedar, and hemlock, and rhododendron. Blueberries are plentiful in season.

This section has one important side trail—the 1.5-mile trail to Buttermilk Falls. Although rather steep in parts, the trail leads to a beautiful waterfall and is well worth the effort.

Road Approaches

Both the northern and southern ends of this section are accessible by vehicle. At the northern end, the Trail crosses U.S. 206 in Culvers Gap, 3.4 miles northwest of Branchville. A parking area is located adjacent to the A.T., 0.3 mile north of the Trail crossing of U.S. 206, on Sunrise Mountain Road just north of its intersection with Upper North Shore Road. At the southern end, the Trail crosses Millbrook-Blairstown Road, 6.2 miles northwest of Blairstown and 1.1 miles southeast of Millbrook Village, a collection of historic buildings. Parking is currently available at the Trail crossing (but may be prohibited in the future).

The Trail in this section also crosses Flatbrookville Road 3.8 miles from the southern end of the section. Vehicle access is available only from the west. Parking is available both 150 feet east and 150 feet west of the Trail crossing. Access from the west is also available at Brink Road, 3.7 miles from the northern end of the section.

Public Transportation

Public transportation is not available at the northern end of this section. Limited bus service to New York City (weekends only), operated by Lakeland Bus Lines, (201) 366-0600, is available in Blairstown, 6.2 miles southeast along Millbrook-Blairstown Road from the southern end.

Maps

For route navigation, refer to Maps Five and Six with this guide. For area detail, refer to the following USGS 7½-minute topographic quadrangles: Culvers Gap, New Jersey-Pennsylvania; Newton West, New Jersey (small corner only); Flatbrookville, New Jersey-Pennsylvania. Other references are NY-NJ TC Trail Maps 16 and 17 (Kittatinny Trails-North and South).

Shelters and Campsites

This section has one shelter:
Brink Road Shelter: Built in 1970; 3.7 miles from northern end of section; 10.9 miles from southern end of section; 900 feet off Trail on dirt road; accommodates 5; wooden floor; water from spring 350 feet beyond shelter on blue-blazed trail.

Next shelter: north 6.8 miles (Gren Anderson Shelter); south 31.1 miles (Kirkridge Shelter in Pennsylvania).

In addition, for thru-hikers, camping is permitted along the Trail on the southern 10 miles of this section, from about 1.0 mile south of Brink Road to Millbrook-Blairstown Road, which pass through the Delaware Water Gap National Recreation Area. It is subject to the following conditions: Camping is permitted only in areas that are more than 0.5 mile from road accesses or the boundaries of the national recreation area. No camping is permitted from 0.5 mile south of Flatbrookville Road to 1.0 mile north of Lake Success

(Crater Lake), where the Wallpack Township-Stillwater Township boundary crosses the Trail (about 2.5 miles north of Flatbrookville Road). Where camping is permitted, hikers must camp not more than 100 feet from the Trail and not less than 200 feet from other campsites. Camping is prohibited within 100 feet of any stream or water source, and any one campsite is limited to 10 persons. No open fires are permitted.

Camping is not permitted along the Trail on the northern 4.5 miles of this section, which pass through Stokes State Forest, except at the Brink Road Shelter.

Supplies and Services

At the northern end of the section, a limited selection of groceries may be obtained at Worthington's Bakery, immediately to the west of the Trail crossing of U.S. 206. A grocery store is located on U.S. 206, 1.6 miles southeast of the Trail crossing. Meals are available at a restaurant 0.1 mile west of the Trail crossing. The Stokes Forest Sport Shop, which sells freeze-dried foods and some camping equipment, is 0.2 mile west. A post office and a laundromat are located in Branchville (ZIP Code 07826), 3.4 miles southeast of the Trail crossing on U.S. 206. At the southern end of the section, groceries, meals, a laundromat, and a post office (ZIP Code 07825) are available in Blairstown, 6.2 miles southeast of the Trail crossing of Millbrook-Blairstown Road.

Public Accommodations

At the northern end of the section, motels are located on U.S. 206, 2.5 miles east and 1.9 miles west of the Trail crossing. At the southern end, motels are located in Blairstown, 6.2 miles to the southeast.

Trail Description, North to South

Miles   **Data**

0.0   From intersection of U.S. 206 and Upper North Shore
       Road (County 636), proceed east on U.S. 206 for 100 feet,

then turn right, cross road, and enter woods on footpath, ascending gradually.

0.2   Turn left onto old woods road, and continue to ascend.

0.4   Trail levels off.

0.6   Cross gravel road, route of gold-and-dark-brown-blazed Acropolis Trail, and resume steady ascent.

0.9   Reach clearing at crest of ridge. Trail turns left, with views to left of U.S. 206 below, then enters woods.

1.4   Reach viewpoint in large cleared area. Culver Lake and U.S. 206 are visible looking back to left, and Culver Fire Tower is visible looking to north along Trail.

2.1   After gradual ascent, reach Jacob's Ladder Trail, with blue-gray markings, which descends about 0.3 mile to right to junction of Coss Road and Woods Road. A.T. ascends gradually, levels off, ascends steadily, and descends briefly.

2.5   Unmarked side trail to left leads to overlook of Lake Owassa.

3.0   Please sign Trail register.

3.1   Pass field of rocks and boulders to left of Trail. Four hundred feet beyond, unmarked side trail to left leads to overlook.

3.3   Begin descent from crest of ridge.

3.7   Reach dirt Brink Road. (Left 0.5 mile to Lake Owassa Road; not passable by car. Right 2.5 miles to Wallpack Center; passable up to 0.2 mile west of Trail crossing.) **Brink Road Shelter** is on right side of road, 0.2 mile to right of Trail crossing. Blue-blazed trail leads to shelter and to spring 350 feet behind shelter, a dependable water source. Trail crosses road, enters woods to right, and begins to ascend.

4.1   Trail levels off, descends slightly, then resumes ascent.

4.4   Reach cleared area on height of ridge. Sweeping views to right of Wallpack Valley, and views through trees to left.

4.5   Reenter wooded area. Trail begins to descend, passing several rock ledges with views to right.

4.8   Turn left on old dirt road, and begin to ascend.

5.1   Turn left off dirt road, and reach rocky, cleared area with views through trees to left. Trail begins to descend.

5.6   Cross short swampy area on rocks, and begin gradual ascent of Rattlesnake Mountain.

6.0   Reach rock outcrop marking summit of Rattlesnake Mountain (1,492 feet), with beautiful views to right. Trail begins to descend, passing through burned-out area with views to right.

6.3   Blue-blazed trail to left leads 200 feet to water source. In another 50 feet on A.T., cross stream. Two hundred feet past stream, Trail turns left and begins to ascend.

6.8   Blue-blazed trail on right leads 75 feet to viewpoint. Trail levels off.

7.4   Reach viewpoint to west from open rocks.

7.6   Turn right onto gravel road. This road was part of the Lake Success second-home subdivision, which was just getting started when the federal government acquired the land for the now-defunct Tocks Island Dam project. Trail continues along gravel roads for next 1.4 miles, with occasional views of Pocono Mountains to west.

7.8   Blue-blazed trail to right descends for 1.5 miles to Buttermilk Falls, a dependable water source. (See description of trail following this section.) In another 125 feet, turn right onto gravel road.

8.7   Turn right onto intersecting gravel road.

9.0   Blue-blazed trail to left leads 150 feet to viewpoint overlooking Crater Lake. Earlier in this century, Crater Lake was a popular summer-cottage colony. The cottages were all razed by the federal government when it acquired the land in the 1960s and 1970s. Fifty feet beyond this point, Trail leaves gravel road and turns right on footpath. In another 150 feet, reach viewpoint to west. Trail turns left, crosses gravel road, and, in another 150 feet, steeply descends face of escarpment. To the right is the Harding Lake Rock Shelter, excavated in the 1940s, which was a temporary home to groups of native American hunters as long ago as 3,000 B.C.E.

9.1   Trail makes right turn. In another 300 feet, cross old gravel road diagonally to right, and reenter woods.

9.4   Pass rock-strewn bog on left.

9.6   Ascend steeply to right of smooth rock.

10.6   Cross dirt road, and turn right on footpath into woods.
10.8   Reach paved Flatbrookville Road. Blue-blazed side trail leads to pump, a tested water source. Trail crosses road, then turns right, and follows paved road for 100 feet, where it turns left on dirt road.
11.1   Trail register is located to right of Trail. Please sign. One hundred and twenty-five feet beyond this point, road to left leads about 125 feet to viewpoint overlooking northern end of Fairview Lake.
11.5   Clearing to left of Trail provides view of Fairview Lake below.
12.4   Dirt road ends. Trail enters woods to left on footpath.
13.8   Reach clearing for powerline. Sand Pond of Camp No-Be-Bo-Sco (Bergen Council, Boy Scouts of America) is visible below to left. Trail turns right after passing powerline tower and follows powerline across ridge for about 0.1 mile. At other side of ridge are views to west of Wallkill Valley and Pocono Plateau. Trail curves to left and reenters woods.
14.0   Descend steeply, then turn left.
14.2   Turn left, skirting north end of swamp, then turn right on dirt road, cross outlet of swamp, and ascend, with swamp to right of Trail.
14.4   Bear right at fork.
14.5   Reach paved Millbrook-Blairstown Road. Turn left, and follow paved road for 0.1 mile.
14.6   Cross paved road, and turn right on woods road (end of section). To continue, proceed south on woods road (see New Jersey Section Six).

Trail Description, South to North

Miles   **Data**

0.0   From intersection of woods road near east side of ridge, proceed northwest along paved Millbrook-Blairstown Road.
0.1   Turn right off paved road, and follow woods road.
0.2   Bear left at fork in road.

0.4   Pass swamp to left of Trail. Trail descends, crosses outlet of swamp, makes sharp left turn away from road, skirting northern edge of swamp, and then curves to right.

0.6   Turn right at fork, and begin steep uphill climb.

0.7   Reach clearing for powerline, with views to left across Wallkill Valley and Pocono Plateau. Follow powerline to right across ridge for about 0.1 mile, then turn left near second powerline tower, and reenter woods. Sand Pond of Camp No-Be-Bo-Sco (Bergen Council, Boy Scouts of America) is visible immediately below. Trail follows crest of ridge on a relatively level path, with views to east.

2.2   After slight descent to left, reach grass-covered dirt road. Follow road for next 1.6 miles, passing several clearings.

3.1   Clearing to right of Trail provides view of Fairview Lake below.

3.5   Road to right leads about 125 feet to viewpoint overlooking northern end of Fairview Lake. Trail register is to left of Trail, 125 feet beyond road. Please sign.

3.8   Reach paved Flatbrookville Road. Trail turns right and follows paved road for 100 feet, where it turns left, crosses road, and reenters woods on footpath. Blue-blazed side trail leads to pump, a tested water source.

4.0   Cross dirt road.

5.0   Descend steeply to left of smooth rock.

5.2   Pass rock-strewn bog on right.

5.4   Cross old gravel road diagonally to right, and reenter woods. In another 300 feet, make sharp left turn, and steeply ascend face of escarpment. To the left is the Harding Lake Rock Shelter, excavated in the 1940s, which was a temporary home to groups of native American hunters as long ago as 3,000 B.C.E.

5.6   One hundred fifty feet beyond top of escarpment, cross gravel road, and reach viewpoint to west. Trail joins gravel road 150 feet beyond viewpoint. Fifty feet beyond this point, blue-blazed trail to right leads 150 feet to viewpoint overlooking Crater Lake. Earlier in this century, Crater Lake was a popular summer-cottage colony. The cottages were all razed by the federal government when it acquired the land in the 1960s and 1970s. Trail continues along gravel roads for next 1.4 miles, with occasional views of Pocono

Mountains to west. These roads were part of the Lake Success second-home subdivision, which was just getting started when the federal government acquired the land for the now-defunct Tocks Island Dam project.

5.9   Turn left onto intersecting gravel road.

6.8   Turn left onto gravel road. One hundred twenty-five feet beyond, a blue-blazed trail to left descends for 1.5 miles to Buttermilk Falls, a dependable source of water. (See description of trail following this section.)

7.0   Leave gravel road, and turn left on footpath into woods.

7.2   Reach viewpoint to west from open rocks.

7.8   Blue-blazed trail on left leads 75 feet to viewpoint. Trail begins to descend.

8.3   Bear right at fork, and, in another 200 feet, cross stream. Immediately past stream, blue-blazed trail to right leads 200 feet to water source. Begin climb of Rattlesnake Mountain, soon passing through burned-out area, with views to left.

8.6   Reach rock outcrop that designates summit of Rattlesnake Mountain (1,492 feet). Beautiful views to left. Begin gradual descent.

9.0   Cross short swampy area on rocks, and begin gradual ascent.

9.5   After reaching rocky, cleared area, with views through trees to right, turn right on old dirt road, and begin to descend.

9.8   Turn right off dirt road, and begin to climb, passing several rock ledges with views to left.

10.1 Reach cleared area on height of ridge. Sweeping views to the left of Wallpack Valley, and views through trees to right.

10.2 Reenter wooded area. Trail descends for 0.1 mile, then ascends slightly, and levels off.

10.3 Begin steeper descent.

10.9 Reach dirt Brink Road. (Right 0.5 mile to Lake Owassa Road; not passable by car. Left 2.5 miles to Wallpack Center; road is passable up to 0.2 mile west of Trail crossing.) **Brink Road Shelter** is 900 feet to left of Trail crossing, on right side of road. Blue-blazed trail leads to shelter and to spring 350 feet behind shelter, a dependable water source. Trail crosses road and enters woods on right, ascending gradually.

11.3   Trail levels off and follows crest of ridge.

11.4   Unmarked side trail to right leads to overlook. Four hundred feet beyond, pass field of rocks and boulders to right of Trail.

11.6   Please sign Trail register.

12.1   Unmarked side trail leads to overlook of Lake Owassa. Shortly afterwards, Trail climbs briefly, descends steadily, then levels off, and continues to descend moderately.

12.5   Reach Jacob's Ladder Trail, with blue-gray markings, which descends about 0.3 mile to left to junction of Coss Road and Woods Road. A.T. ascends gradually, then descends slightly, and levels off.

13.2   Reach viewpoint in large cleared area. Culver Lake and U.S. 206 are ahead on right. Culver Fire Tower is visible straight ahead. Trail reenters woods, descends for 0.1 mile, then levels off, with several brief ascents and descents.

13.7   Reach clearing, with view of U.S. 206 to right. Trail turns right and begins steady descent.

14.0   Trail crosses gravel road, route of gold-and-dark-brown-blazed Acropolis Trail, and levels off for 0.2 mile, then resumes steady descent on old woods road.

14.4   Turn right, leaving old woods road, and continue to descend.

14.6   Cross U.S. 206, and turn left. Continue along U.S. 206 for 100 feet to intersection of U.S. 206 and Upper North Shore Road (County 636), end of section. To continue, cross Upper North Shore Road, and enter woods (see New Jersey Section Four).

Buttermilk Falls Trail

This blue-blazed trail descends a vertical distance of about 1,000 feet to the base of Buttermilk Falls. The first part of the trail is quite steep, but, after about 0.3 mile, the grade moderates. A dirt road is crossed at 0.5 mile. At 1.3 miles, the trail descends very steeply for 400 feet. At the end of this descent, the top of the falls is 200 feet to the right of the trail, providing a dependable water source. The trail turns left and, after a short, steep descent at 1.6 miles, reaches Mountain Road. The base of the falls is 0.2 mile to the right along the road. Total one-way distance to top of falls is 1.5 miles; to base of falls, 1.9 miles. Allow 45 minutes for descent to top of falls; 60 minutes for return.

Millbrook-Blairstown Road to Delaware Water Gap
New Jersey Section Six
13.6 Miles

Brief Description of Section

This section follows the ridge of the Kittatinny Mountains until the Trail descends to cross the Delaware River at the Delaware Water Gap. The northern part of this section lies within the boundaries of the Delaware Water Gap National Recreation Area, while the southern part passes through Worthington State Forest. From the northern end of the section (1,260 feet), the Trail climbs to the Catfish Fire Tower (1,565 feet), then follows the Kittatinny Ridge, passing Sunfish Pond, a beautiful glacial lake. Many beautiful views can be seen along the Trail on both sides of the ridge. After descending along Dunnfield Creek, the Trail reaches the Delaware River, at the Delaware Water Gap. It crosses the river on the I-80 highway bridge (350 feet).

The Delaware Water Gap was a popular resort area as early as 1850. By the 1890s, many large hotels had sprung up. Most of the hotels had vanished by the 1950s, but the gap still attracts throngs of tourists who come to see its geological splendor.

In 1962, Congress authorized the construction of a dam across the Delaware River at Tocks Island, about five miles north of the Delaware Water Gap. This dam would have flooded much of the Wallpack Valley along the Delaware River. Several years later, the Delaware Water Gap National Recreation Area was established to provide recreational facilities at the lake that would have been created by the Tocks Island Dam. Strong opposition to the dam by conservation groups and local residents resulted in the project being repeatedly postponed, and the dam was finally deauthorized in 1992. One beneficial result of the project was that the land acquired by the federal government for the national recreation area has provided the Trail with a protected corridor.

Toward the southern end of this section, blue- and red-blazed trails lead to the summit of Mt. Tammany (1,527 feet), which offers a magnificent view of the gap. (See description of these trails following this section.) Many other trails also intersect the A.T. in this area. For descriptions of these trails, see the *Delaware Water Gap National Recreation Area Hiking Guide*, published by the New York-New Jersey Trail Conference.

Road Approaches

Both the northern and southern ends of this section are accessible by vehicle. At the northern end, the Trail crosses Millbrook-Blairstown Road, 6.2 miles northwest of Blairstown and 1.1 miles southeast of Millbrook Village, a collection of historic buildings. Parking is available at the Trail crossing. At the southern end, the Trail crosses the Delaware River on the I-80 toll bridge at the Delaware Water Gap. No parking is available at the Pennsylvania side of the Delaware River bridge; however, ample parking is provided at the Delaware Water Gap National Recreation Area Information Center on the New Jersey side of the bridge, 1.0 mile from the southern terminus of the section. Additional parking is available at the Dunnfield Creek Natural Area, 1.4 miles from the southern end of the section, where the Trail leaves paved roads and begins its climb to the Kittatinny Ridge. Motorists approaching from the east should exit I-80 before crossing the bridge, at the sign marked "Rest Area." Those coming from the west should take the first exit after crossing the bridge into New Jersey.

Public Transportation

Limited bus service to New York City and to other points via Martz Trailways, (800) 233-8604, is available at Delaware Water Gap, Pennsylvania, at the southern end of this section. Limited bus service to New York City (weekends only), operated by Lakeland Bus Lines, (201) 366-0600, is available in Blairstown, 6.2 miles southeast along Millbrook-Blairstown Road from the northern end of this section.

Maps

For route navigation, refer to Map Six with this guide. For area detail, refer to the following USGS 7 ½-minute topographic quadrangles: Flatbrookville, New Jersey-Pennsylvania; Bushkill, Pennsylvania-New Jersey; Portland, New Jersey-Pennsylvania; Stroudsburg, Pennsylvania-New Jersey. Other references are NY-NJ TC Trail Maps 15 and 16 (Kittatinny Trails-South).

Shelters and Campsites

No shelters are located in this section.

Two designated campsites are in the southern portion of this section, which passes through Worthington State Forest. *Campsite No. 1* is 0.5 mile west of the Trail, 3.0 miles from the southern end of section. *Campsite No. 2* is on the Trail, 4.6 miles from the southern end of section. No water is available at either of these campsites. Camping at these sites is subject to the following restrictions: No ground fires are permitted. Camping is limited to one night. Groups are limited to 10 persons. In addition, a developed campground is located at the Delaware River, 2.2 miles from the Trail along a woods road that departs from the Trail 4.6 miles north of the southern end of this section (fee charged for camping). Camping is prohibited in Worthington State Forest, except at those designated sites.

Camping for thru-hikers is permitted in the Delaware Water Gap National Recreation Area (from about 1.8 miles north of Sunfish Pond to the northern terminus of this section), subject to the following restrictions: Camping is permitted only in areas that are more than 0.5 mile from road accesses or the boundaries of the national recreation area. Hikers must camp not more than 100 feet from the Trail and not less than 200 feet from other campsites. Camping is prohibited within 100 feet of any stream or water source, and any one campsite is limited to 10 persons. No open fires are permitted.

Supplies and Services

Meals, groceries, and other supplies may be obtained in the village of Delaware Water Gap, Pennsylvania (ZIP Code 18327), at the southern end of the section. The Presbyterian Church of the Mountain provides an information center for hikers. At the northern end of the section, groceries, meals, a laundromat, and a post office (ZIP Code 07825) are available in Blairstown, 6.2 miles to the southeast.

Public Accommodations

Motels are available in Delaware Water Gap, Pennsylvania, at the southern end of the section, and in Blairstown, New Jersey, 6.2 miles southeast of the northern end of the section. The Presbyterian Church of the Mountain in Delaware Water Gap operates a hostel for hikers.

Trail Description, North to South

Miles	Data
0.0	Trail turns off paved Millbrook-Blairstown Road and continues on gravel road to south.
0.3	Road makes sharp turn to right.
0.4	Make sharp left turn off gravel road, and ascend on footpath through rhododendron thicket, as orange-blazed Rattlesnake Swamp Trail continues straight ahead on road. Rattlesnake Spring, a dependable water source, is on left side of road, 50 feet beyond A.T. turnoff. Trail follows old woods road for short distance, then turns left on footpath.
0.6	Turn left onto gravel road. In another 275 feet, turn off road, and reenter woods on footpath to right.
0.7	Turn right on gravel road, and ascend to Catfish Fire Tower.
1.0	Reach Catfish Fire Tower (built in 1922) and small adjacent building (1,565 feet). Sixty-foot-high tower offers

splendid 360-degree view. Trail reenters woods and continues on relatively level footpath, with views through trees to left.

2.0   Trail comes out at southeast side of ledge and runs for short distance along rim, with good views to left. Orange-blazed Rattlesnake Swamp Trail goes off to right and leads in about 0.5 mile to Catfish Pond.

2.1   Trail comes out on rim for second time.

2.7   Begin descent to Camp Road.

3.3   Cross dirt Camp Road (formerly known as Mohican Road), and reenter woods to left. In another 50 feet, cross Yards Creek, a water source, and begin to ascend, often steeply.

3.4   Red-blazed Coppermines Trail begins to right.

3.6   Reach end of steep section. Trail continues to ascend on moderate grade.

4.8   View to left of Trail of storage ponds for the Yards Creek pumped-storage generating station.

5.3   Reach grassed-over Kaiser Road, which comes in from right. (The road is named for the Keyser family, who owned land and mineral rights in the area.) Continue ahead on old road.

5.5   Turn right off woods road, and continue on footpath, with views to right. (Road descends mountain to southeast, with spring 0.3 mile down slope.)

5.8   Enter Worthington State Forest.

6.0   Reach viewpoint. To left are storage ponds for Yards Creek pumped-storage generating station. Directly behind, Catfish Fire Tower may be visible between ridges.

6.1   Powerline crosses Trail, with views on both sides of ridge.

6.3   View west (over trees) toward Pennsylvania at open area. Trail begins to descend.

6.7   Cross brook, and begin to ascend.

7.4   Turn right at double blaze.

7.6   Blue-blazed Garvey Springs Trail to right leads 600 feet to Garvey Springs, a seasonal water source, and continues for 1.2 miles to River Road (Old Mine Road).

7.7   Reach eastern end of Sunfish Pond. No camping permitted near pond. To left, Turquoise Trail leads 0.4 mile along east shore of pond to Sunfish Pond fire road. A.T. continues along shore of pond on rocky footpath.

8.1   Cross outlet of pond.

8.4   Reach western end of Sunfish Pond, where Sunfish Pond fire road meets the A.T. Monument to right of Trail notes that the Sunfish Pond Natural Area has been designated a registered national landmark. Continue along woods road.

9.0   Reach **Campsite No. 2** (no water). Turn left off woods road, and continue on footpath. Road straight ahead, which is blue-blazed Douglas Trail (named after Supreme Court Justice William O. Douglas, an ardent conservationist), leads 1.7 miles to developed **campground** in Worthington State Forest along Delaware River.

10.6   After passing through burned-out area (starting to regenerate), reach trail junction. Yellow-blazed Beulahland Trail to right leads to **Campsite No. 1** in 0.5 mile (no water) and Fairview Parking Area on River Road (Old Mine Road) in 1.3 miles. Unmarked Holly Springs Trail to left leads 0.2 mile to Holly Springs, a water source (may fail in dry weather), and continues for another 0.2 mile to the Dunnfield Creek Trail. A.T. continues straight ahead, descending gradually.

11.7   Blue Dot Trail to Mt. Tammany (see description on page 179) and green-blazed Dunnfield Creek Trail come in from left. A.T. continues along right bank of Dunnfield Creek, still descending.

12.0   Turn left off woods road, and, in 200 feet, cross wooden bridge over Dunnfield Creek.

12.1   Reach parking area and pump, a tested water source. Trail continues through parking area.

12.2   At end of parking area, turn left along paved road. Continue along road for 250 feet, then make right turn at underpass, and go under I-80. (Red Dot Trail to Mt. Tammany begins at parking area straight ahead on paved road. See description on page 179.)

12.3   At other side of underpass, turn right, and continue along paved road parallel to I-80.

12.6   Pass Trail register (please sign) and Delaware Water Gap National Recreation Area Information Center (water, restrooms, picnic area, boat launching, and parking). Continue along paved road.

12.9   Cross bridge over Delaware River into Pennsylvania.

13.6   Section ends where dead-end street comes in from left before toll plaza. To continue, turn left onto dead-end street. Description of A.T. continues in the *Appalachian Trail Guide to Pennsylvania*.

Trail Description, South to North

Miles   **Data**

0.0   Turn right at the end of dead-end street onto sidewalk along I-80, and cross bridge over Delaware River.

0.7   After crossing bridge, continue along service road, which parallels I-80.

1.0   Pass Trail register (please sign) and Delaware Water Gap National Recreation Area Information Center (water, restrooms, picnic area, boat launching, and parking). Continue along paved road parallel to I-80.

1.3   Turn left at underpass, and go under I-80. Make left turn at other side of underpass, and continue along paved road for about 250 feet. (Red Dot Trail to Mt. Tammany begins at parking area to right of underpass. See description on page 179.)

1.4   Turn right into parking area at sign, "Dunnfield Creek Natural Area." Trail continues through parking area.

1.5   Pass pump, a tested water source. Trail leaves parking area and enters woods.

1.6   Turn left, and cross wooden bridge over Dunnfield Creek. Two hundred feet past bridge, Trail turns right on woods road and continues along left bank of Dunnfield Creek.

1.9   Take left fork, and continue on woods road, as Blue Dot Trail to Mt. Tammany and green-blazed Dunnfield Creek Trail begin to right. (See description of Blue Dot Trail on page 179.) Continue gradual ascent toward Sunfish Pond.

3.0   Reach trail junction. To left, yellow-blazed Beulahland Trail leads to **Campsite No. 1** in 0.5 mile (no water) and Fairview Parking Area on River Road (Old Mine Road) in 1.3 miles. To right, unmarked Holly Springs Trail leads 0.2 mile to Holly Springs, a water source (may fail in very dry weather), and continues for another 0.2 mile to Dunnfield

Creek Trail. A.T. continues, with area burned out several years ago (starting to regenerate) noticeable to right of Trail. Ridge of Kittatinny Mountains is also visible to right of Trail.

4.6   Reach **Campsite No. 2** (no water) at junction with woods road. Trail turns right on road. Road to left (blue-blazed Douglas Trail, named after former Supreme Court Justice William O. Douglas, an ardent conservationist) leads 1.7 miles to developed **campground** in Worthington State Forest along Delaware River.

5.2   Reach Sunfish Pond. Monument to left of Trail notes that the Sunfish Pond Natural Area has been designated a registered national landmark. No camping permitted near pond. Trail continues along left shore of pond, while woods road (Sunfish Pond fire road) goes around right shore.

5.5   Cross outlet of pond. In another 350 feet, turn right at double blaze.

5.9   Pass east end of pond. To right, Turquoise Trail leads 0.4 mile along east shore of pond to Sunfish Pond fire road.

6.0   Blue-blazed Garvey Springs Trail to left leads 600 feet to the Garvey Springs, a seasonal water source, and continues for 1.2 miles to River Road (Old Mine Road).

6.2   Turn left at double blaze. Shortly afterwards, start descent to brook.

6.9   Cross brook.

7.3   View west (over trees) toward Pennsylvania at open area.

7.5   Powerline crosses Trail. Views on both sides of ridge. Reach crest of ridge. To right, note storage ponds for Yards Creek pumped-storage generating station. Delaware River is visible to left. Directly ahead, Catfish Fire Tower may be visible between ridges.

7.8   Leave Worthington State Forest, and enter Delaware Water Gap National Recreation Area.

8.1   Reach old grassed-over Kaiser Road. (The road is named for the Keyser family, who owned land and mineral rights in the area. To right, road descends mountain to southeast. Spring is 0.3 mile down slope.) Continue ahead on old road.

8.3   Take right fork of trail. Kaiser Road continues to left, leading to old copper mines.

8.8   View to right of Trail of storage ponds for the Yards Creek pumped-storage generating station.

9.3   Trail turns left at double blaze.

10.0 Start steeper descent to Camp Road.

10.2 Red-blazed Coppermines Trail begins to left.

10.3 Cross Yards Creek, a source of water, then immediately cross dirt Camp Road (formerly known as Mohican Road). Trail reenters woods to left and begins ascent of Kittatinny Ridge.

10.9 Reach top of ridge, with views along Trail to right.

11.5 Trail comes out on southeast side of ledge and runs for short distance along rim, with good views to right.

11.6 Trail comes out on rim for second time. Orange-blazed Rattlesnake Swamp Trail goes off to left and leads in about 0.5 mile to Catfish Pond.

12.6 Reach Catfish Fire Tower (built in 1922) and small adjacent building. Sixty-foot-high tower offers splendid 360-degree view. Begin descent to Millbrook-Blairstown Road along gravel road.

12.9 Leave gravel road, and follow footpath to left.

13.0 Turn left on gravel road for 275 feet, then turn off road, and reenter woods on footpath to right.

13.2 Turn right on old woods road at powerline. Pass through rhododendron thicket, then turn right onto gravel road. (Orange-blazed Rattlesnake Swamp Trail goes left on road.) Fifty feet to left on road is Rattlesnake Spring, a dependable water source.

13.4 Road makes sharp turn to left.

13.6 Reach paved Millbrook-Blairstown Road (end of section). To continue, turn left along road (see New Jersey Section Five).

Mt. Tammany Trails

Two side trails lead from the A.T. to the summit of Mt. Tammany, from which there are splendid views over the Delaware Water Gap and west into Pennsylvania.

The Red Dot Trail begins at the parking area near the I-80 underpass, 1.3 miles from the southern end of the section. It ascends steadily but at a moderate rate, except for one short, steep climb. The Blue Dot Trail turns off the A.T. 1.9 miles from the southern end of the section, crosses Dunnfield Creek, and ascends gradually to the summit. Both trails join at the summit and can be combined to make a scenic loop.

Table of Distances

Unless otherwise noted, the mileage points below reflect the point at which a walker first encounters the road or other feature, depending on the direction of travel. For example, in New York Section 2, the A.T. includes a 0.3-mile roadwalk on Hurds Corners Road—the southbound hiker begins it 6.6 miles from the northern end of the section, but the northbound hiker begins it 6.9 miles from the northern end.

North to South Sec. Cum. Miles			South to North Cum. Sec. Miles	
		N.Y. Section 2		
0.0	0.0	Hoyt Road, N.Y./Conn. State Line	161.8	7.1
1.0	1.0	Duell Hollow Road	160.8	6.1
1.2	1.2	**Wiley (Webatuck) Shelter**	160.6	5.9
1.6	1.6	Leather Hill Road	160.2	5.5
6.6	6.6	Hurds Corner Road	154.9	0.2
7.1	7.1	N.Y. 22	154.7	0.0
		N.Y. Section 3		
0.0	7.1	N.Y. 22	154.7	7.0
2.4	9.5	County 20 (West Dover Road)	152.3	4.6
3.1	10.2	**Telephone Pioneers Shelter** (0.1 mile on side trail)	151.6	3.9
3.4	10.5	West Mountain Summit	151.3	3.6
3.9	11.0	Penny Road	150.8	3.1
7.1	14.1	N.Y. 55	147.7	0.0
		N.Y. Section 4		
0.0	14.1	N.Y. 55	147.7	7.2
0.3	14.4	Old N.Y. 55	147.4	6.9

2.2	16.3	Depot Hill Road	145.5	5.0
3.3	17.4	**Morgan Stewart Memorial Shelter**	144.4	3.9
		(75 feet on side trail)		
3.4	17.5	Mt. Egbert Summit	144.3	3.8
5.8	19.9	I-84 Overpass, Mountain Top Road	141.8	1.3
7.2	21.3	N.Y. 52	140.5	0.0

N.Y. Section 5

0.0	21.3	N.Y. 52	140.5	4.8
1.6	22.9	Hosner Mountain Road	138.9	3.2
1.9	23.2	**Bailey Spring Campsites**	138.6	2.9
		(0.4 mile on side trail)		
4.8	26.1	Taconic State Parkway	135.7	0.0

N.Y. Section 6

0.0	26.1	Taconic State Parkway	135.7	7.2
0.3	26.4	Hortontown Road, **RPH Shelter**	135.4	6.9
2.7	28.8	Long Hill Road	133.0	4.5
3.1	29.2	Shenandoah Mountain Summit	132.6	4.1
7.2	33.3	N.Y. 301, Canopus Lake	128.5	0.0

N.Y. Section 7

0.0	33.3	N.Y. 301, Canopus Lake	128.5	7.4
2.1	35.4	Sunk Mine Road	126.4	5.3
3.6	36.9	**Dennytown Road Campsites**	124.9	3.8
7.4	40.7	Canopus Hill Road	121.1	0.0

N.Y. Section 8

0.0	40.7	Canopus Hill Road	121.1	5.0
0.7	41.4	Canopus Hill Viewpoint	120.4	4.3
1.7	42.4	Chapman Road	119.4	3.3
2.5	43.2	Denning Hill Viewpoint	118.6	2.5
4.4	45.1	Old West Point Road	116.7	0.6
5.0	45.7	U.S. 9, N.Y. 403	116.1	0.0

N.Y. Section 9

0.0	45.7	U.S. 9, N.Y. 403	116.1	5.8
3.4	49.1	South Mountain Pass	112.7	2.4
3.6	49.3	**Hemlock Springs Campsite**	112.5	2.2
5.1	50.8	N.Y. 9D, Westchester-Putnam County Line	111.0	0.7
5.8	51.5	Bear Mountain Bridge (west end)	110.3	0.0

N.Y. Section 10

0.0	51.5	Bear Mountain Bridge (west end)	110.3	13.3
0.6	52.1	Bear Mountain Inn	109.7	12.7
2.6	54.1	Bear Mountain Summit	107.6	10.6
4.2	55.7	Seven Lakes Drive	106.1	9.1
5.8	57.3	**West Mountain Shelter** (0.6 mile on side trail)	104.5	7.5
7.0	58.5	Palisades Interstate Parkway	103.3	6.3
7.7	59.2	Black Mountain	102.5	5.5
9.1	60.6	**Brien Memorial Shelter**	101.2	4.2
11.1	62.6	Seven Lakes Drive	99.2	2.2
13.3	64.8	Arden Valley Road	97.0	0.0

N.Y. Section 11

0.0	64.8	Arden Valley Road	97.0	5.5
1.1	65.9	**Fingerboard Shelter**	95.9	4.4
3.2	68.0	Lemon Squeezer	93.7	2.2
5.5	70.3	N.Y. 17	91.5	0.0

N.Y. Section 12

0.0	70.3	N.Y. 17	91.5	12.0
1.1	71.4	Arden Mountain Summit	90.4	10.9
1.8	72.1	Orange Turnpike	89.7	10.2
3.2	73.5	East Mombasha Road	88.3	8.8
4.9	75.2	West Mombasha Road	86.5	7.0
6.1	76.4	Mombasha High Point	85.4	5.9

8.1	78.4	Fitzgerald Falls	83.4	3.9
8.4	78.7	Lakes Road	83.1	3.6
9.9	80.2	**Wildcat Shelter**	81.6	2.1
		(0.1 mile on side trail)		
10.2	80.5	Cat Rocks	81.3	1.8
10.7	81.0	Eastern Pinnacles	80.8	1.3
12.0	82.3	N.Y. 17A	79.5	0.0

N.Y. Section 13

0.0	82.3	N.Y. 17A	79.5	5.9
5.4	87.7	Prospect Rock	74.1	0.5
5.9	88.2	State Line Trail	73.6	0.0

N.J. Section 1

0.0	88.2	State Line Trail	73.6	9.6
1.1	89.3	Long House Creek	72.5	8.5
2.2	90.4	Long House Road	71.4	7.4
3.6	91.8	Warwick Turnpike	70.0	6.0
4.0	92.2	**Wawayanda Shelter**	69.6	5.6
		(0.1 mile on side trail)		
5.1	93.3	Iron Mountain Road Bridge	68.5	4.5
6.3	94.5	Barrett Road	67.3	3.3
8.2	96.4	Wawayanda Mountain	65.5	1.5
9.6	97.8	N.J. 94	64.0	0.0

N.J. Section 2

0.0	97.8	N.J. 94	64.0	11.6
2.2	100.0	County 517	61.0	8.6
4.6	102.4	County 565	59.4	7.0
5.8	103.6	Pochuck Mountain Summit	58.2	5.8
7.4	105.2	**Pochuck Mountain Shelter,**		
		(0.1 mile on side trail)	56.6	4.2
7.8	105.6	Wallkill Road	56.2	3.8
10.1	107.9	Wallkill River Bridge	53.9	1.5
11.6	109.4	N.J. 284	52.4	0.0

N.J. Section 3

0.0	109.4	N.J. 284	52.4	9.9
1.0	110.4	Lott Road (Jersey Avenue)	51.4	8.9
2.0	111.4	Unionville Road (County 651)	50.4	7.9
3.3	112.7	Goodrich Road	49.1	6.6
4.3	113.7	Gemmer Road	48.1	5.6
6.1	115.5	Courtwright Road	46.3	3.8
6.9	116.3	County 519	45.5	3.0
8.2	117.6	**High Point Shelter**	44.2	1.7
		(0.1 mile on side trail)		
9.9	119.3	N.J. 23	42.5	0.0

N.J. Section 4

0.0	119.3	N.J. 23	42.5	14.3
2.5	121.8	**Rutherford Shelter**	40.0	11.8
		(0.4 mile on side trail)		
5.3	124.6	Deckertown Turnpike	37.2	9.0
5.5	124.8	**Mashipacong Shelter**	37.0	8.8
8.0	127.3	Crigger Road	34.5	6.3
8.9	128.2	Sunrise Mountain Summit	33.6	5.4
11.2	130.5	**Gren Anderson Shelter**	31.3	3.1
		(0.3 mile on side trail)		
12.3	131.6	Culver Fire Tower	30.2	2.0
14.3	133.6	U.S. 206	28.2	0.0

N.J. Section 5

0.0	133.6	U.S. 206	28.2	14.6
3.7	137.3	**Brink Road Shelter**	24.5	10.9
		(0.2 mile on side trail)		
6.0	139.6	Rattlesnake Mountain Summit	22.2	8.6
7.8	141.4	Buttermilk Falls Trail	20.4	6.8
10.8	144.4	Flatbrookville Road	17.4	3.8
14.6	148.2	Millbrook-Blairstown Road	13.6	0.0

N.J. Section 6

0.0	148.2	Millbrook-Blairstown Road	13.6	13.6
1.0	149.2	Catfish Fire Tower	12.6	12.6
3.3	151.5	Mohican Road	10.3	10.3
7.7	155.9	Sunfish Pond	5.2	5.2
9.0	157.2	**Campsite No. 2** (no water)	4.6	4.6
10.6	158.8	**Campsite No. 1**	3.0	3.0
		(0.5 mile on side trail–no water)		
12.2	160.4	Dunnfield Creek Parking Area	1.4	1.4
13.6	161.8	Delaware Water Gap, Pa.	0.0	0.0

Index